PENGUIN BUSINESS
ACTION!

Vivek Mashrani, CFA, is a founder and director at TechnoFunda Ventures, based out of Ahmedabad, India. He is also building a community under his TechnoFunda initiative to help people become better investors. Previously, he served at the Bengaluru and London offices of HSBC as AVP in their investment banking as well as strategy teams.

Vivek is a CFA charter holder and member of the CFA Society India, and an MBA in capital markets from Narsee Monjee Institute of Management Studies (NMIMS), Mumbai. He is a strong believer in lifelong learning, networking and collaboration.

Anand Venkitachalam is a founder and managing partner at KARM Capital, where wealth meets purpose in a harmonious blend of financial stewardship and meaningful impact. He is also the founder and CEO of Nuvolance Technologies Pvt. Ltd, which offers SAAS-based tools for community collaboration, such as Dhruva and Polaris.

Anand holds an MTech from IIT Bombay and an executive MBA from IIM Bangalore. He has over twenty-five years of experience working in leadership roles at high-tech engineering MNCs and holds eleven patents. He is also an Art of Living volunteer, teaching and practising mindfulness techniques.

T0282056

ACTION!

100

POWERFUL PRINCIPLES OF

PERSONAL
FINANCE

VIVEK MASHRANI
ANAND VENKITACHALAM

PENGUIN
BUSINESS

An imprint of Penguin Random House

PENGUIN BUSINESS

USA | Canada | UK | Ireland | Australia
New Zealand | India | South Africa | China | Singapore

Penguin Business is part of the Penguin Random House group of companies
whose addresses can be found at global.penguinrandomhouse.com

Published by Penguin Random House India Pvt. Ltd
4th Floor, Capital Tower 1, MG Road,
Gurugram 122 002, Haryana, India

First published in Penguin Business by Penguin Random House India 2024

ISBN 9780143463436

Typeset in Adobe Caslon Pro by MAP Systems, Bengaluru, India
Printed at Replika Press Pvt. Ltd, India

www.penguin.co.in

Disclaimer

are not responsible for, the content, accuracy, or legality of any linked sites or resources.

Changes to Information:

The author and the publisher reserve the right to modify, update, or remove any information in this book without notice. It is the responsibility of the reader to verify the currency and accuracy of any information before relying on it.

No Endorsement:

References to specific products, services, or companies in this book do not constitute an endorsement or recommendation by the author or the publisher.

By reading this book, the reader acknowledges and agrees to the terms of this disclaimer.

Contents

Section 5: Optimize (O)

Section 6: Navigate (N)

Introduction

India, a land of incredible cultural diversity, has seen monumental economic shifts over the last several decades. Thanks to an expanding middle class and digitization efforts that have transformed the economy, personal finance is no longer seen as optional; rather, it has become essential. Unfortunately, however, much of India remains unaware of or uneducated on how best to manage their funds, leading to missed opportunities or, worse, financial crises.

Traditional Indian settings typically limited money discussions to the four walls of the home and savings primarily focused on gold and fixed deposits. While these remain viable forms of investment even today, India's financial landscape has significantly expanded. We now have access to an abundance of financial instruments, from stocks to cryptocurrency, and the markets now demand a deeper understanding of finance for optimal investment planning. Our planning strategy for our savings must be constantly on our minds.

Given the vast range of options and the rapid expansion of the financial markets in the country, it has never been more essential than now that every Indian understands personal finance. Financial literacy not only safeguards our funds but also leverages our hard-earned money towards the creation of wealth. But we live in an age where peer pressure dictates our spending decisions, which are based on short-lived social trends.

Financial literacy will help us make sound decisions based on sound logic rather than short-term trends.

This book has been developed specifically for Indian audiences and addresses the distinct financial challenges, opportunities and cultural considerations that exist here in our great nation. As you embark upon this journey of self-improvement by learning about personal finance, you will come to see that personal finance isn't about numbers alone but also about going beyond market fluctuations and realizing dreams, securing the future and attaining peace of mind.

Personal finance information can be overwhelming; every day we are bombarded with advice from financial experts on television, articles on our social media feeds and well-intentioned advice from friends and family members. While all this advice may be useful, it also often leads to information overload, resulting in what's known as analysis paralysis, in which it becomes hard to know which advice applies specifically to our circumstances or needs. That is where this book shines—not simply as another source of financial advice but instead as an actionable playbook tailored specifically for Indian audiences.

Sports are an apt analogy for investing too. Take, for instance, a cricket team's approach to an important match. While its players possess the required foundational skills, success often lies in how well the playbook addresses the opposition players, the pitch conditions and the team strengths. Likewise, the aim of this book is not merely to impart foundational knowledge but also to supply precise strategies that take into account India's unique financial landscape, respect its cultural nuances and the Indian investor's familial duties and aspirational goals.

Furthermore, playbooks imply actionable steps. Unlike theoretical guides that linger on the fringes, this book delves deep into how personal finance works. It is not about simply giving you knowledge on how to save or invest. This book provides practical examples, actionable templates and clear guidance, all of which are designed to take the reader far beyond mere understanding to move towards real implementation.

Additionally, personal finance should never be approached passively. As life changes and one's goals and circumstances evolve too, this playbook provides guidance to the reader for every life stage, whether it is to do with a career, a start-up, the first home purchase, saving for the children's college education or retirement preparation. This guide offers essential support for everyone.

In an age when financial products and platforms are evolving quickly, one can easily be seduced by trendy financial advice or succumb to myths that compromise long-held principles. This playbook serves as a grounding device. It offers both traditional wisdom and modern insights in equal measure, bringing you back to tried-and-tested principles while equipping you to navigate new financial frontiers successfully.

At its heart, this book is not about personal finance—it's about empowerment. As an invaluable companion on your path to financial freedom, this playbook can serve as your road map and companion in shaping it proactively rather than reactively.

Book Theme: ACTION towards Mastery in Personal Finance

Assess (A): Assessing oneself is key to any successful financial journey, just as one cannot set forth anywhere without knowing where one's starting point is and what the current circumstances are. Without an accurate picture of one's financial health or status, one cannot create an effective plan and establish goals to move towards. An effective assessment goes well beyond simply tallying assets and liabilities; rather, it involves exploring your financial goals, risk tolerance and any personal habits that might influence your future monetary decisions. Family responsibilities being an essential component of the Indian way of life, you would have to consider obligations like supporting your ageing parents or funding a child's college education. By carefully considering your financial standing in relation to the culture you live in and the norms it observes, an appropriate financial plan that best serves your unique circumstances will emerge.

Create a plan (C): Once you understand where you stand financially, the next step would be to develop an actionable strategy to guide the direction of your savings plan. A personalized approach should be tailored to address both your financial goals and the constraints unique to India—festivals, social norms and unexpected expenses. So this plan needs to be both robust and flexible in order for you to succeed financially. From saving for a Diwali vacation to retirement planning, having a good plan in place is critical for achieving financial success!

Take action (T): Plans that are not followed up by action can only remain wishes. Taking the first steps towards implementing your plan requires discipline, commitment and sometimes, sacrifices from you. They could mean investing in mutual funds, cutting out unnecessary expenses or setting up an emergency fund. In India, taking this step might mean breaking traditional financial practices such as festival shopping. With time and dedication, these actions will lay the foundation for a prosperous future.

Inspect progress (I): India's dynamic economy keeps the financial landscape constantly shifting, necessitating periodic check-ins on your journey in order to make sure you remain on the correct course. To remain successful financially, regularly inspect your investments' performance, analyse your spending patterns and re-evaluate your financial goals in line with the changes in India's diverse investment opportunities and economy. This way you will ensure that you not only stay true to your plan but also adapt it in keeping with any unexpected events.

Optimize (O): Personal finance offers many opportunities that you can use to optimize your investments. This could mean the refinancing of loans, changing their terms, or adjusting your investment portfolio allocations to take full advantage of the tax-saving opportunities exclusive to Indian tax law. Optimization of your investments ensures that every rupee spent or earned works towards fulfilling your financial goals effectively and efficiently.

Navigate (N): Navigating your way through the arena of personal finance can be an unpredictable journey that features numerous twists, turns, roadblocks and potential detours. To do this in the complex Indian economic environment of today demands resilience, adaptability and continuous learning so that you can stay the course and meet your financial aspirations and goals despite any unexpected obstacles or emergencies that may arise along your journey.

In sum, ACTION is more than just an acronym. It's a philosophy, a structured approach designed to empower every Indian to take charge of his or her financial future. In your journey through the pages of this book, ACTION will become your compass, guiding you through the intricate world of personal finance tailored for the citizen of the vibrant and diverse land that is India.

Special message to the reader . . .

As you open this book and embark on your transformational journey, allow us to share an important message. Our experiences offer insight and hope, both of which should inspire anyone looking to realize their financial destiny.

First and foremost, allow us to extend our sincerest congratulations: simply picking up this book is evidence that you want to take control of your financial future. In such a vast and varied country as India, where multiple cultural, family and societal considerations influence our financial decisions, making the effort towards self-education in personal finance is both commendable and essential.

From the tales told to us by grandmothers to regional myths and folk stories, we've long been reminded of the value of hard work and persistence in building wealth. Unfortunately, few stories explore the subject of managing, growing and protecting the wealth we work so diligently to get. This book seeks to fill that gap. Yet, ultimately it will be your passion, dedication and persistence that will determine whether these lessons become real-world knowledge for you or simply remain empty words on paper.

Financial freedom can be achieved much the way spiritual journeys are undertaken across our great nation—through reflection, discipline and enlightenment gained along the journey. Your path may include market volatility, personal emergencies that necessitate spending, or holiday sales tempting you to make impulse purchases. Yet, like pilgrims who remain focused on reaching their shrine, so too you must remain dedicated in your pursuit of financial independence. That will open many doors of possibility, both for yourself and your loved ones.

The financial world may seem complex at first, with terms like equity, mutual fund or cryptocurrency sounding foreign to many of us. But remember, every expert was once just starting out! Even we struggled with some unfamiliar terms ourselves at one time, before eventually getting to know them in our financial quest—just like they can for you too.

As the journey towards financial freedom is uniquely individual, the exact results one gets from applying what the book says will vary. While the guidelines, strategies and insights have been tailored for an Indian audience and will prove useful for most readers, the results they can bring will depend on the person reading the book. Each reader will have his or her own unique goals, dreams, responsibilities and aspirations that constitute their idea of financial freedom. Your financial plan must reflect all of your unique goals.

As you journey down this financial road, you may face criticism or advice from well-meaning friends or family members offering unsolicited suggestions. While listening is key, keep your ears and mind open but remember to trust in yourself, your knowledge, your research and your instincts. Your financial journey belongs solely to you—become its most ardent advocate.

As you dive deeper into the world of personal finance, we urge you not to lose sight of the bigger picture. Money may be powerful and essential, but ultimately its use should serve a higher purpose—the experiences it funds, the peace of mind it brings or the legacies it creates are purposes worth prioritizing.

Financial literacy may seem like just another thread of life's intricate tapestry; yet, when put to use strategically and thoughtfully, it can add vibrancy, strength and beauty to one's life.

Here's wishing you clarity of vision, strength of resolve and joy at every milestone passed on the path towards financial freedom! May your journey be as fruitful and enjoyable as its final destination itself!

With warmest wishes and utmost faith,
Vivek Mashrani, CFA and Anand Venkitachalam

Section 1: Assess (A)

'By failing to prepare, you are preparing to fail.'
—Benjamin Franklin

The first step to achieving financial freedom is to assess your current financial situation. This would include an understanding of what your income, expenses, loans and assets are. By creating a detailed budget, you can identify areas where you can reduce your expenses and increase your savings. An assessment of your current financial situation is the foundation for creating a plan that will lead you to your financial goals.

Chapter 1

Assess Income and Expenses

'Don't depend on a single income. Make an investment to create a second source.'

—Warren Buffett

Bank statement

Bank statements provide an extensive account of individual or organizational financial transactions over an established time period. Bank statements in India, as elsewhere, serve as valuable resources to individuals and corporations for analysis of their various sources of income, which will help with personal financial planning, tax filing and loan applications.

Types of income

1. Salary income

For employed people, the salary is often the primary source of income and is usually credited directly into their bank accounts each month. To identify it on your statement, look out for credits with descriptions like 'SALARY' or the name of the employer. Additionally, keep an eye out for any bonuses, incentives or allowances that may be included as part of your salary package.

2. Interest income

This consists of income earned from savings accounts, fixed deposits, recurring deposits or from any other investments paying you an interest. To locate it in your passbook, search for the names of financial institutions and entries under 'INT', 'INTEREST' or 'INT/INTEREST'. Also take note of whether the interest credits occur monthly, quarterly or annually.

3. Dividend income

Companies pay their shareholders dividends as an incentive for investing in their stock. To spot dividend income on a bank statement, look out for entries against terms such as 'DIV', 'DIVIDEND', or for the name of the company paying the dividend. Dividends may be issued quarterly, semi-annually or annually, so pay attention to when these credits appear and also when these credits could appear again.

4. Rental income

Rental income can be earned by leasing your residential or commercial property to tenants and would feature in your bank statement under 'RENT', 'LEASE', or the name of the tenant. Usually rental income means monthly credits, but the frequency of rental payments would depend on your lease agreement terms with your client and could be different.

5. Freelance or consulting income

Consulting income can be earned for professional services on an agreed-upon contract. To identify this revenue, look out for descriptions such as 'CONSULTING', 'FREELANCE', or the name of the client in your passbook. The frequency of payments would depend on contract terms or project completion schedules.

6. Business income

This consists of money earned from running a business or by providing goods and services. Business income may come in different forms and from multiple sources over time. When searching for yours in your passbook, look out for entries under 'SALES', 'REVENUE' or the customer's name. Remember that this income could come from multiple sources.

7. Capital gains

Capital gains are realized upon the sale of stocks, mutual funds or property at a profit. To identify capital gains on a bank statement, look out for references like 'SALE', 'CAPITAL GAIN', or the name of the asset sold. The frequency of entries would, of course, depend on one's investment activities.

8. Pension or annuity income

This type of income is received as part of one's retirement benefits or insurance policies, such as through pension funds or company policies for retirement purposes. To find this type of income, search for the term 'PENSION', 'ANNUITY' or the name of the fund/company concerned. Typically, this form of revenue will be received monthly or annually.

9. Other sources of income

Additional income sources could come in the form of gifts, winnings and inheritances that do not fit neatly into any one category listed above. To identify such sources of income, look out for terms such as 'GIFT' or 'WINNING', or the names of organizations providing these. Remember that this type of income has irregular payment cycles and the amounts too will be uncertain.

10. Foreign income

This can take various forms, from payments received from working abroad and serving international clients directly, or as passive income generated from investments overseas. To identify this source of revenue in your bank statement, look for terms like 'FOREIGN REMITTANCE', 'FOREIGN INCOME', or the name of any entity/individual paying this type of money. The frequency of the amounts credited could fluctuate, as could the amounts themselves, on account of exchange rate changes.

11. Government subsidies or benefits

These are forms of financial support given by the government under various social welfare or economic development schemes. To identify government subsidies in a bank statement, look out for terms like 'GOVT SUBSIDY', 'GOVT BENEFIT', or the name of specific schemes run by governments. Payments could be monthly, quarterly or annual, depending on the nature of the scheme.

12. Loan or credit disbursements

These are received from financial institutions as loans or advances that must be repaid with interest over time. While technically not considered income, they can still be identified on your bank statement as inflows of funds. Look out for 'LOAN DISBURSEMENT', 'CREDIT ADVANCE', or the name of a lending institution from which you expect such disbursements.

Bank statements provide invaluable insights into an individual's or organization's financial activities. A careful reading of them will reveal your income from various sources, which is necessary for financial planning, filing of tax returns and loan applications. Therefore, when reviewing bank statements, it's essential to affirm that all sources of revenue are fully and correctly reported and accounted for.

Types of expenses

Expenses are an indispensable aspect of everyday life, representing the costs we incur to meet our desires, needs and dreams. Understanding where we spend allows us to better manage our finances and make informed spending decisions. Here we present an exhaustive list of the various heads of expenses and the sources that will provide you information on them.

1. Housing

One of the primary costs associated with living can be housing costs. Rent/loan payments, property taxes, homeowners' insurance premiums and maintenance, and electricity, water, gas and other utility bills can quickly add up.

2. Transportation

Transportation expenses can include car loans and payments, fuel expenses, vehicle maintenance and repair bills, parking fees and public transit fares (like bus or metro fare).

3. Food

Groceries, dining out and ordering food can all add up quickly when budgeting for food expenses. Food expenses may also be incurred during special events that involve social gatherings.

4. Health

Health-related expenses typically consist of health insurance premiums, co-payments or deductibles associated with visits to the doctor, purchase of medicines, medical procedure costs, dental and vision-care costs as well as the purchase of wellness products designed to enhance one's overall well-being.

5. Education

Education expenses cover tuition fees, textbooks, supplies and technology, school transportation costs and extracurricular activities, both as part of formal education (such as at schools or universities) and as self-improvement courses. This category should also encompass formal vocational education or professional certification programmes that help individuals further their careers and aid their personal advancement.

6. Debt repayments

This category encompasses loan payments such as home loans, student loans, personal loans and credit card bills.

7. Utilities

Beyond housing-related utilities, utilities would also cover expenses related to Internet and cable services, and landline or mobile phone bills.

8. Personal care expenses

These include expenses on products and services associated with personal hygiene and grooming, like toiletries and grooming products, hair-cutting or salon services, beauty and skincare products and clothing.

9. Entertainment expenses

These would include spends on movies, concerts, sporting events, theme parks, vacations and subscription services such as Netflix or Spotify.

10. Insurance

Beyond health insurance and homeowner's/renter's insurance policies, other forms of insurance coverage also contribute significantly to expenses. Examples may include life, auto, travel and pet policies in addition to various liability policies.

11. Taxes

Income, property and other forms of government-imposed taxes.

12. Childcare expenses

These would include day-care fees, babysitting services, educational supplies and after-school programmes or activities.

13. Gifts and donations

This category encompasses expenses on gifts bought for people on their birthdays, weddings and other special events, as well as charitable donations or contributions to causes or organizations.

14. Subscriptions and memberships

Monthly and yearly subscription costs for magazines, newspapers, gym memberships, professional organizations and other services add up quickly over time to significantly pad up expenses.

15. Home maintenance costs

Apart from regular housing expenses, repairs, renovations and furniture or appliance purchases also account for significant outlays in maintaining the home.

16. Pets

Costs associated with owning and caring for animals, such as expenses on food, veterinary services, grooming sessions and accessories.

17. Miscellaneous

This category encompasses expenses which do not fall into any one of the previous categories, including bank fees, legal costs, professional services fees, license or permit costs and unexpected or emergency expenses.

Understanding and categorizing expenses by type can help you develop a budget and prioritize your spending. Tracking your expenditure and finding ways to cut costs in each category allows for informed financial decision-making, which leads to long-term financial success. Keep this in mind for efficient management of expenses. Keeping track of your expenses is vitally important!

Categories of income

Once you've identified all your sources of income from your bank statements, categorizing them based on their regularity and your level of involvement in obtaining them is key to better comprehending your finances and making sound financial planning decisions. Here is an outline for putting your income sources into four groups—regular, one-time, active and passive:

1. Regular income

Regular income can be defined as earnings received on an ongoing basis, such as monthly, quarterly or yearly payments from various sources and which can reasonably be expected to continue for some time to come. Examples of regular income sources are salary, interest (from savings accounts or fixed deposits), rent, pension, etc.

2. One-time income

'One-time' refers to something that does not occur regularly, and such income should not be relied upon for long-term financial planning. Examples of one-time income are gifts, inheritances, capital gains from selling property or investments, winnings from lotteries or gambling, etc.

3. Active income

Active income consists of earnings generated as a result of direct effort or labour on your part and may require a significant investment of time and energy in order to be generated. Common examples of active income are salary income, consulting income or commission income from sales or referrals.

4. Passive income

This comprises earnings generated without your direct involvement or effort, often stemming from prior investments of time, money or resources that continue to produce returns without needing ongoing maintenance efforts from you. Examples of passive income are interest income from savings, accounts, fixed deposits or bonds, dividend income, rental income and royalties from intellectual property (such as books, music or patents).

To categorize your income sources, review your bank statement and categorize each income entry in it as regular or one-time, depending on its recurrence and predictability. Next, evaluate whether an income requires your active involvement or is generated passively. Some income may fall into multiple categories, depending on their nature and your personal considerations.

By classifying your income sources into Regular, One-time, Active and Passive streams, you can gain an easier grasp on your total annual earnings.

Case study: Sankaran Pillai—Calculation of Annual Income

Background

Here we calculate the annual income of Sankaran Pillai, an individual working as a software engineer in Chennai.

1. Salary income

Sankaran relies heavily on his salary when it comes to his income. His annual salary amounts to a total of Rs 9,34,400 after all deductions, including taxes.

2. Additional allowances

In addition to his basic salary, Sankaran also receives additional allowances, including Rs 1600 in transport allowance per month.

3. Income from residential property

Sankaran owns and rents out a residential property to get a rental income of Rs 2 lakh annually.

4. Investment income

Sankaran's fixed deposits in the bank provide him monthly interest earnings of Rs 2000 while stocks provide him an annual dividend of Rs 10,000.

Calculation of Sankaran's total annual income:

Source of Income	Monthly Amount (Rs)	Annual Amount (Rs)
Salary		9,34,400
Other allowances	1600	19,200
Residential property		2,00,000
Interest	2000	24,000
Dividends		10,000
Total		**11,87,600**

Sankaran's total annual income is Rs 11,87,600 (Rupees eleven lakh eighty-seven thousand and six hundred).

Categories of expenses

Categorizing expenses under Needs, Desires and Dreams can help you better organize and allocate your resources and plan your outgo more effectively. This approach allows you to distinguish between essential expenses, such as those on utilities or loan payments, non-essential but desired purchases, such as tickets for entertainment shows, and long-term goals, which require saving for future success. Here is how you can categorize your expenses:

1. Needs

These expenses cover your basic necessities of life, which would include: housing (rent or loan payments), utilities (electricity, water, gas), groceries and basic household supplies, transportation (public transportation, fuel, vehicle maintenance, insurance), healthcare (insurance premiums, medications, doctor visits), basic clothing, insurance (life, health, home, or vehicle) and debt repayments (loans, credit card balances).

Analyse your bank and credit card statements carefully to isolate all the necessary expenses, then allocate enough funds in your budget plan to cover these basic needs.

2. Desires

These make for non-essential expenses that make life more pleasurable or comfortable but may cost a lot in terms of money or resources. They can be reduced or cancelled altogether in order to save money for allocation towards more pressing needs. One's desires may be for products or services like dining out or ordering food, entertainment (movies, concerts, streaming subscriptions), hobbies and leisure activities, travel and vacations, electronic items, gadgets, or non-essential home appliances and gifts for friends and family.

As part of your financial review, identify any discretionary expenses you may have and review them to see if they align with your long-term goals. If necessary, reduce these expenditures in order to allocate more funds towards meeting needs or fulfilling your dreams.

3. Dreams

Dreams are ambitious financial goals that may require long-term planning, savings and investments in order to fulfil them. Dreams may include significant life milestones or purchases. They may include buying a home or investing in real estate, starting a business or pursuing a new career path, or your own higher education, early retirement or financial independence, luxury vacations or once-in-a-lifetime experiences or charitable giving or philanthropy.

Establish your dream goals and estimate their associated costs, then develop a savings or investing plan over time to reach these milestones. Regularly assess your progress towards meeting them so that your budget and your spending habits can be modified appropriately.

To effectively categorize your expenses under Needs, Desires and Dreams, follow these steps:

1. Review expenses that you have recorded as 'categorizable expenses' on both your bank and credit card statements, as discussed earlier.
2. Define three new categories for expenses: Needs, Desires and Dreams.
3. Evaluate each existing head of expense to identify which category it falls under. For instance: housing, utilities and groceries would fall under Needs; dining out, entertainment and travel under Dreams, etc.
4. Revamp your budget, allocating funds according to your priorities and financial goals, then make the changes necessary to meet them while still enjoying some discretionary spending on your desires.
5. Review your spending regularly in order to remain within your budget and reach your financial goals.

By categorizing expenses into needs, desires and dreams, you can gain a clearer sense of your financial priorities and make informed decisions regarding allocation of your resources. This approach helps balance your essential costs with what is to be set aside for your aspirational goals.

Case study: Ashish Gupta—Categorization of Annual Expenses

Background

In this case study, we will assess Ashish Gupta, who works as a financial analyst in Indore. His expenses will be divided into the three categories—needs, desires and dreams—for ease of analysis and prioritization of financial goals.

1. Needs

Needs refer to the essential expenses necessary for basic living, such as for one's survival and for maintaining a decent standard of living. For Ashish, this might mean expenses on food and transportation, which he would need for survival and to maintain his decent quality of life. Let's look at Ashish's needs below:

a) *Housing:* Ashish pays an annual rent of Rs 2,40,000 for his apartment
b) *Utilities:* Ashish's annual spend on utilities (electricity, water and gas bills) is approximately Rs 30,000
c) *Food and groceries:* Here, Ashish's annual expenditure stands at Rs 1,80,000
d) *Transportation:* Ashish's annual expenses related to fuel, maintenance and public transport amount to Rs 60,000

Ashish's total annual expenses on needs amount to Rs 5,10,000 per annum.

2. Desires

Desires refer to expenses not necessary for one's survival, but which provide comfort, entertainment and leisure. They add to one's quality of life! Ashish's desires and the expenses they entail are:

    a) *Entertainment:* Ashish allocates Rs 50,000 per year for movies, concerts and leisure activities

    b) *Travel:* Ashish sets aside Rs 1 lakh annually for vacations and for exploring new destinations

    c) *Dining out and socializing:* Ashish's expenses on these counts is annually around Rs 60,000

    d) *Fitness and hobbies:* Ashish sets aside Rs 30,000 annually for gym memberships and the pursuit of his hobbies

Ashish's total annual expenses on desires is Rs 2,40,000.

3. Dreams

Long-term dreams are typically related to personal growth or major life milestones, such as education, and require careful financial planning for their fulfilment. Let's consider some of Ashish's aspirations here:

    a) *Higher education:* Ashish plans to pursue a master's degree and allocates Rs 1,50,000 per year towards tuition fees and related expenses

    b) *Starting a business:* Ashish sets aside Rs 1,50,000 per year as investment towards his entrepreneurial dream

Ashish's total annual dream expenses amount to Rs 3,00,000.

Summary of Ashish's annual expenses:

Our analysis of Ashish's annual expenses provides the following breakdown:

- Expenses on Needs: Rs 5,10,000
- Expenses on Desires: Rs 2,40,000
- Expenses on Dreams: Rs 3,00,000

Ashish must strike a balance between fulfilling his needs, desires and dreams while remaining financially stable. By understanding his spending patterns and prioritizing his financial goals, he can make informed decisions that can help him achieve both his dreams while also fulfilling his needs. Regular review and adjustment of expenses will enable him to manage his finances efficiently for optimal financial well-being.

Analyse your cash flow

Personal cash flow management refers to the practice of planning, organizing and tracking income and expenses to reach one's financial goals, maintain financial stability and improve one's overall well-being. Successful personal cash flow management involves several essential components:

1. Understanding your income

Identify all your sources of income, such as salary, rental income, investment returns and side hustles, to understand and track them effectively in order to gauge your overall financial capabilities and set appropriate financial goals. This will give you an accurate picture of where you stand financially today and help you set attainable financial objectives for the future.

2. Tracking your expenses

Monitor all expenses, such as rent, loan payments and insurance premiums as well as variable expenses like groceries, entertainment and clothing purchases. Understanding where your money goes can help you identify your spending patterns or pinpoint areas where savings can be made.

3. Calculating your net cash flow

To calculate your net cash flow, simply subtract your expenses from your income. If this number is positive, it indicates a surplus, and if negative, it indicates a deficit from costs exceeding earnings.

4. Creating a cash flow statement

Using either spreadsheet software or personal financial software to develop your cash flow statement, outline your income and expenses by category as well as your net cash flow for any specified period (i.e., monthly or annually).

5. Analysing patterns

You should review your cash flow statement closely in order to detect patterns between income and expenses and search for ways in which your spending can be reduced or your income raised.

6. Crafting a budget

Create a realistic budget aligned with your financial goals, taking into account both income and expenses. Allocate funds for your necessities, savings, investments and debt repayments to create an optimal plan for yourself and your future financial goals.

7. Adjusting your spending habits

Evaluate and adapt your spending patterns so they align with the priorities set in your financial plan and budget. This could involve cutting out non-essential expenses or finding additional avenues of income generation.

8. Establishing short- and long-term financial goals

Set short- and long-term financial goals, such as creating an emergency fund, closing a debt or saving for retirement. These will serve to guide your decisions and keep the focus on what's most important.

9. Creating an emergency fund

Savings accounts can serve as emergency funds to cover unexpected expenses or unexpected loss of income, so consider setting aside three to six months' living expenses as your emergency savings fund goal.

10. Prioritizing debt repayment

Prioritize repayment of high-interest debts first in order to lower your overall borrowing costs and create an effective debt repayment plan that fits your budget and aligns with your financial goals.

11. Saving and investing

Set aside part of your income as savings and for investing. Consider long-term strategies, such as retirement accounts or diversified portfolios, to grow your wealth over time.

12. Reviewing and adjusting your plan

Regularly review your cash flow, budget and financial goals to account for changes in your financial circumstances, priorities or goals. Make adjustments as required.

13. Utilizing financial tools and resources

Use personal finance software, mobile apps or spreadsheets to track and manage your cash flow effectively. Seek professional guidance from a financial planner/adviser, should you require any further advice or personalized recommendations.

By regularly managing your personal cash flow, you can take control of your finances, make informed decisions and strive for a secure financial future.

Savings

Savings are an integral component of personal financial management and consist of that portion of your income set aside for later use. A savings rate measures the percentage of income saved over an established time frame. Maintaining an effective savings rate can ensure financial security, fulfilment of goals and the building of wealth.

Regular and diligent savings constitute the foundation of sound financial planning. Accumulating funds for emergencies, investments, education and retirement is crucial for creating long-term security. Regular savings create financial protection during unexpected situations while building lasting financial security for the future. Managing one's savings consistently and diligently is vitally important for long-term planning success.

People's savings rates vary, based on individual circumstances, financial goals and income levels. Financial planning experts generally suggest that one strives to save 20 per cent or more of one's income. However, finding an optimal savings ratio between saving more money than needed and meeting immediate financial obligations remains key. Higher-income earners might be able to set aside larger portions while those on lower salaries might start small and gradually build up their savings over time.

Individuals looking to increase their savings rate can use various strategies. The diligent tracking of income and expenses is key in order to identify areas where savings could increase.

Creating and sticking to a budget can assist in managing expenses effectively, and prioritizing savings over discretionary purchases is also beneficial in getting a sizeable savings fund sooner rather than later.

Automating savings by setting up an automatic transfer of money from one's salary account to one's savings or investment accounts can make saving easier and consistent, eliminating the temptation to spend money before it can be saved. Exploring ways of passive income generation, such as from investments, rental properties or dividend-paying stocks, may further accelerate savings over time.

To maximize savings, it's also essential to adopt a frugal mindset and practise mindful spending. Making conscious choices to cut discretionary expenses, such as cable TV subscriptions and non-essential purchases, while searching for cost-cutting alternatives, will contribute significantly towards increasing one's savings rate. Renegotiating bills regularly, as well as searching out discounts or promotions, may also save money over time.

Individuals must frequently re-evaluate their savings rate as their income and financial goals change, especially as income rises. As more money arrives for savings, it is advisable that one increases one's savings rather than immediately raising one's expenses.

Increased savings rates over time can accelerate your progress towards your financial goals.

You can build a strong foundation for your long-term financial security through savings alone.

Chapter 2

Assess Assets and Liabilities

Types of Assets

Individuals and businesses have various types of assets. Assets may accumulate gradually, leading to greater net worth and financial security over time. Here we explore some popular types of assets in India.

1. Financial Assets

One method of building assets is to invest in various types of financial instruments, like stocks, mutual funds, fixed deposits, government bonds or retirement accounts like Employee Provident Fund (EPF) or Public Provident Fund (PPF). These variously offer capital appreciation opportunities, dividend income or interest earnings. To build an asset base gradually over time, individuals must carefully select their investments, based on their risk tolerance, time horizon and financial goals.

Saving money in fixed deposits and savings accounts at banks or post offices can be an efficient and low-risk method to build assets. While the returns may be modest compared with the returns from other investment avenues, fixed deposits provide liquidity and capital-preservation benefits.

Contributing to retirement accounts such as an EPF, PPF or National Pension System (NPS) can assist individuals in creating long-term assets for retirement. Not only do these investments provide tax benefits, but they also call for savings discipline over time while creating substantial assets, ensuring financial security for the investor post-retirement.

2. Real estate

Owning and investing in real estate properties is an increasingly popular asset-building strategy in India. The properties could be residential apartments, commercial buildings, land or even agricultural land. Real estate can appreciate over time while simultaneously yielding rental income, offering long-term capital appreciation potential as well as providing security through ownership of tangible assets that provide long-term security and peace of mind.

3. Gold and precious metals

Indians have long recognized gold as an asset worth holding as it represents both storage of value and potential appreciation, providing protection from inflation and economic uncertainty. Silver and platinum could also be taken into consideration for diversification of one's precious-metals portfolio.

4. Intellectual property

Intellectual property such as patents, copyrights and trademarks can be extremely profitable assets in today's knowledge-based economy. They can generate licensing fees or royalties and produce significant financial advantages for both individuals and businesses alike.

5. Art and collectibles

Art, antiques, rare coins, stamps or other collectables can serve as valuable assets that appreciate over time and offer diversification opportunities. Art can provide aesthetic value and serve as a form of personal expression while potentially yielding financial returns.

6. Business ownership

A business that you own and operate can be an immensely valuable asset. Entrepreneurs and business owners have the chance to amass assets through their business operations. The profits generated from the business can be reinvested to purchase additional assets, expand operations or diversify into different ventures, creating significant wealth over time through appreciation in business value as well as through the cash flows generated.

7. Equity in start-ups

Start-ups typically offer equity stakes to investors, who can then participate in their success. Successful ventures may result in considerable asset appreciation and wealth creation.

Note that the suitability and potential risks of different types of investments would vary for different individuals, depending on their financial goals, risk tolerance and investment horizon. Seek professional financial advice and conduct thorough research before making your investment decisions. A diversified portfolio that is regularly monitored can contribute towards long-term wealth creation and financial security.

Case study: Priya Roy—Asset Allocation

Background

Priya Roy is forty-five years old and has been working as an IT professional for the last twenty years. She has consistently allocated 70 per cent of her income towards her living expenses and short-term financial goals, while 30 per cent is allocated for asset accumulation to secure her financial future. Priya's consistent savings of 30 per cent of her income over twenty years has grown her assets to Rs 2.5 crore today. Her asset acquisition journey:

1. Financial Assets

Priya invests 10 per cent of her assets in fixed deposits and high-interest savings accounts as emergency reserves, providing herself access to liquidity through these accounts. Their combined current value is Rs 25 lakh. In addition, 10 per cent of her assets have been invested in debt mutual funds for added protection against possible market crashes.

Priya allocates 10 per cent of her assets towards retirement planning. Through automatic deductions from her salary and voluntary contributions, she invests 5 per cent of her assets in an EPF and another 5 per cent in an NPS.

Priya's total investment in debt instruments is 30 per cent of her assets with a combined value of Rs 75 lakh.

Priya invests 15 per cent of her assets in equity mutual funds and 5 per cent in individual stocks. Her total investments in equities are 20 per cent of her assets with a combined value of Rs 50 lakh.

2. Real estate

Priya has made significant investments in real estate, which accounts for 40 per cent of her assets. Her residential apartment is valued at Rs 1 crore.

3. Gold

Priya has invested Rs 25 lakh in gold-based investments; half of this is held in physical form and the remainder in the form of Sovereign Gold Bonds (SGBs).

Percentage allocation of assets:

Sr. No.	Type of Asset	% Allocation	Value (Rs)
1	Real Estate	40	1.00 crore
2	Equity	20	0.50 crore
3	Debt	30	0.75 crore
4	Gold	10	0.25 crore
			2.50 crore

Priya's investment portfolio illustrates an asset allocation approach with diversification at its heart, prioritizing long-term wealth creation over short-term goals. By diversifying her assets across different asset classes, Priya hopes to build up her savings, secure her financial future and meet her long-term ambitions.

Types of Liabilities

Individuals may incur liabilities through various sources, resulting in financial obligations and debts. The liabilities may arise in relation to personal, professional or legal circumstances and should therefore not be discounted. Here are some common types of liabilities:

1. Loans

This is the primary type of liability most individuals living in India take on. They have the obligation to make regular repayments (with interest included) of the loan in instalments, according to the terms agreed upon with their lender. Various kinds of loans exist:

a) Personal Loans

These are taken for meeting one's personal needs, such as medical costs, education expenses or wedding costs.

b) Home loans

Home loans enable individuals to purchase or construct residential properties. These loans are long-term liabilities and involve regular repayments.

c) Vehicle loans

Vehicle loans are for the purchase of cars, motorcycles or other forms of transport, such as bus. Payment arrangements generally involve fixed monthly instalments.

d) Education loans

These loans are taken to cover higher-education expenses. Many of these loans come with advantageous repayment terms to assist individuals in their quest for education.

e) Gold loans

They are secured loans where individuals pledge their gold assets as collateral to borrow money. These loans are commonly used for short-term financial needs.

2. Credit card debt

Nowadays, credit cards have become indispensable in our lives and are also an increasing source of liabilities when not used responsibly. Individuals using them incur debt when they make purchases on them and must make timely repayments to avoid incurring interest and late-payment fees that accrue during each billing cycle. Credit card liabilities arise when individuals carry balances forward from cycle to cycle, and it's crucial that individuals use instruments such as the credit card responsibly, making timely repayments so as to limit their liabilities as much as possible. It is crucial that they make full and on-time payments of their outstanding amounts against their card to prevent further liabilities from accruing.

3. Overdrafts

Individuals may access overdraft facilities from banks. The overdraft facility allows individuals to withdraw more funds than are available in their bank accounts, up to an agreed-upon limit. Like personal lines of credit, overdrafts create liabilities as they require individuals to repay both the borrowed amounts plus any applicable interest charges. Proper management of this facility must take place in order to avoid excessive liabilities.

4. Individual tax liabilities

People may owe taxes to the state or Central government, based on their income. Taking responsibility for one's own tax liabilities means calculation and payment of taxes and deadline compliance in filing returns. Penalties, fines or legal ramifications may arise if any taxes are overdue. Hence, it's critical that individuals fulfil all their tax responsibilities while maintaining accurate records in compliance with the tax regulations.

5. Personal guarantees

Individuals may offer personal guarantees as an insurance on behalf of family, friends or business partners to secure credit. Such guarantees devolve on the individual if the borrower defaults, making him/her financially responsible for the non-payment of dues against the credit. Individuals should carefully assess the risks before providing personal guarantees to others.

6. Legal liabilities

Individuals may face legal liabilities stemming from legal disputes, lawsuits or judgments brought against them. Liabilities could stem from contractual issues, personal injury claims, property-related matters and/or any legal obligation. Legal liabilities could even require significant financial outgo on legal fees awarded by courts or settlement payments to others.

An essential aspect of financial well-being lies in the responsible management of liabilities, so individuals need to assess their capacity, budget efficiently and make timely repayments to minimize their burdensome liabilities while remaining healthy financially. Consulting a professional for advice as well as becoming familiar with the different kinds of liabilities that they can be subjected to will enable individuals to make more informed financial decisions.

Case study: Manjula Anand—Computing Liabilities

Background

Manjula Anand, a thirty-year-old working professional in Coimbatore, carries various financial obligations and liabilities that have accrued during her professional life. By exploring Manjula's case, we can get an idea of what kind of financial liabilities can beset individuals.

1. Home loan

Manjula purchased her house five years ago using a home loan of Rs 50 lakh for a term of twenty years from a bank. Her regular equated monthly instalments (EMIs) amounted to Rs 41,800, including both principal and interest components. This was a long-term liability.

2. Personal loan

Manjula has taken a personal loan of Rs 3 lakh for a term of two years to finance a family wedding. Personal loans usually carry higher interest rates than traditional loans, and her personal loan meant a monthly EMI of Rs 14,100.

3. Car loan

Manjula recently purchased a new car with the help of a Rs 7 lakh loan from a bank, to be repaid over five years. This entails a monthly repayment of Rs 14,500.

4. Credit card debt

Over the years, Manjula has accumulated credit card debt by using her credit cards for various expenses. She has outstanding balances on multiple credit cards, including monthly interest charges and additional liabilities, and they cumulatively amount to Rs 50,000. She has to focus on repaying her credit card debts at the earliest.

5. Education loan

Manjula enrolled for higher studies some time ago, for which she took an education loan of Rs 10 lakh, making for monthly instalments of Rs 10,000 as repayment until such time the loan was fully repaid. She recognizes this loan as an outstanding debt till such time as it will be fully cleared.

6. Tax liabilities

As an independent individual with income tax liabilities, Manjula needs to calculate and pay her annual taxes by their due dates. Her current total salary is Rs 47,20,000 per annum; hence her annual income tax liability is about Rs 12 lakh.

7. Personal guarantees

Manjula stood as guarantee for her brother's business loan of Rs 10 lakh from a bank. Manjula's brother later defaulted on the loan, leaving her responsible for its repayment under their personal guarantee agreement.

8. Legal liabilities

Recently, Manjula became embroiled in a legal dispute over a property she had purchased. As soon as the matter reached the courts, legal fees and associated costs became her liability; these financial burdens added to her existing financial repayment commitments. Any payments or associated penalties that may arise as part of the litigation proceedings could range from Rs 1 lakh to Rs 5 lakh, or even more.

Conclusion

Manjula's case highlights the various sources of liability that an individual in Indian society may have to contend with. She has both long-term and short-term liabilities. Her long-term liabilities consist of a home loan of Rs 50 lakh, while short-term liabilities consist of personal loans amounting to Rs 3 lakh, a car loan of Rs 7 lakh, credit card debts of Rs 50,000, an education loan of Rs 10 lakh, tax liabilities of Rs 12 lakh and legal costs of anywhere between Rs 1 lakh and Rs 5 lakh.

Manjula must responsibly manage her liabilities to maintain a healthy financial standing, budget effectively, make payments on time and prioritize debt repayments and debt reduction as part of her overall liability reduction strategy. Professional advice and sound financial strategies can assist Manjula in effectively handling her liabilities and attaining financial stability.

Net worth

Net worth is an essential financial indicator that gives an in-depth snapshot of an individual's overall financial health. It measures the difference between an individual's assets and liabilities. An asset inventory is taken, from which the liabilities are subtracted. Here is what it involves:

Step 1: Calculation of Total Assets

Step 2: Assessment and calculation of Total Liabilities

Step 3: Calculation of Net Worth

The formula is as follows:

Net Worth = Total Assets - Total Liabilities

Step 4: Analysis of the Result

The result will represent your net worth, which presents an overview of your financial standing, which in turn can be evaluated against one's goals. A positive net worth means that assets outweigh liabilities, and a negative net worth indicates that liabilities outstrip assets.

Step 5: Regular Monitoring

It is crucial that your net worth is regularly assessed as your financial circumstances evolve over time. You need to assess your progress, adjust your financial strategies accordingly and make informed decisions on your savings, investments and debt reduction. Revisit this calculation periodically and view the result against your goals to evaluate your savings strategies or debt reduction options.

Calculating your individual net worth is an insightful exercise that gives you an accurate representation of your financial health. Make sure to update this calculation frequently and use the results to guide you to informed financial decisions that match up with your long-term goals, helping you increase your net worth over time and achieve financial stability.

Case study: Pavan Uppara—Computing Net Worth

Background

Pavan Uppara is a forty-year-old working professional living in Jaipur who has acquired various assets and liabilities over his lifetime. Here we calculate his net worth.

Assets:

1. *Real estate:* Pavan owns a house whose estimated market value is Rs 75 lakh

2. *Financial assets*

   a) Savings account: Pavan maintains a savings account with a balance of Rs 5 lakh
   b) Fixed deposits: He has one fixed deposit worth Rs 10 lakh
   c) Mutual funds: Pavan had invested Rs 5 lakh in various mutual funds, which are currently valued at Rs 7 lakh
   d) Stocks: He owns stocks valued at Rs 5 lakh

3. *Vehicle:* Pavan's vehicle has an estimated market value of Rs 8 lakh
4. *Provident Fund (PF) account:* Pavan's contribution to his provident fund account through his employment currently stands at Rs 6 lakh
5. *Gold and jewellery:* Pavan owns gold and jewellery valued at approximately Rs 4 lakh

Liabilities:

   1. *Home loan:* Pavan has a home loan with an outstanding balance of Rs 45 lakh
   2. *Personal loan:* His outstanding balance on his personal loan is Rs 3 lakh
   3. *Car loan:* Pavan has an outstanding balance of Rs 6 lakh on his car loan agreement
   4. *Credit card debts:* Pavan accumulated credit card debts amounting to Rs 1 lakh

Net worth calculation:

To determine Pavan's net worth, we subtract his total liabilities from his total assets.

	Assets	Amount (in Rs lakh)	Liabilities	Amount (in Rs lakh)
1	Real estate	75	Home loan	45
2	Savings account	5	Personal loan	3
3	Fixed deposits	10	Car loan	6
4	Mutual funds	7	Credit card debt	1
5	Stocks	5		
6	Vehicle	8		
7	PF	6		
8	Gold	4		
	Total Assets	**120**	**Total Liabilities**	**55**

Net Worth Calculation = Total Assets − Total Liabilities
    = Rs 120 lakh − Rs 55 lakh
    = Rs 65 lakh

Pavan's net worth is Rs 65 lakh.

Chapter 3

Assess Risk

Risk and reward

Risk and reward are fundamental concepts in individual financial planning, so understanding their interrelationship is vital for making informed investment decisions to achieve one's long-term financial goals. Here is an overview of the risks and rewards of individual financial planning:

Risks in financial planning

'Risk' refers to the potential for loss or variability in investment returns. All investments carry some level of risk; different investment choices come with differing degrees of associated risks. Some of the common forms of investment risk are market risk, credit risk, inflation risk, etc.

These risks will be covered in detail in the subsequent section of this chapter.

Rewards

'Reward' refers to the anticipated return or gain that an investor can expect from his/her investments. Rewards from investments can vary, based on how risky the investments are. Investments carrying greater risk generally yield larger potential rewards, while investments that offer lesser risks generally offer smaller yields. Some of the common investment vehicles offering potential returns are:

a) **Stocks:** Shares of a company represent ownership in that entity and offer capital appreciation as well as dividend income opportunities. Stocks have historically seen higher returns than debt, but also carry increased market risks.

b) **Bonds:** Bonds are debt instruments issued by governments, municipalities or corporations to finance their expenditure. Bonds typically provide fixed interest payments over a definite term before returning the principal at maturity, as opposed to stocks, which usually provide higher returns but carry more risk.

c) **Mutual funds:** Mutual funds pool money from multiple investors to invest in a diversified portfolio of stocks, bonds and other assets. They offer capital appreciation potential and income potential at various levels of risk, depending on each fund's investment strategy.

d) **Real estate:** Real estate investments offer potential for rental income, property value appreciation and tax benefits, not to mention stable cash flows. In fact, this asset can generate solid cash flows despite the potential liquidity or market risks.

e) **Alternative investments:** These would include assets such as private equity, hedge funds, commodities or venture capital that typically offer greater risk-return profiles and may allow investors to diversify their holdings with investments that bring potentially higher returns.

Overview of the basic risks

There are various essential risks when it comes to individual financial planning, and one should be mindful of them so that one may create comprehensive yet resilient plans. Here's an overview of some of the basic risks that individual finance planning entails:

1. Market risk

This refers to the possibility of investment losses caused by fluctuations in the financial markets, which typically impact individuals who have invested in stocks, bonds, mutual funds or other market-based instruments. Economic conditions or geopolitical events, as well as changing investor sentiment, could lead to market fluctuations. To mitigate market risk, it's essential that investments be diversified after due risk-tolerance assessment. Keeping a long-term perspective will help.

2. Credit risk

When investing or lending money, investors and loan officers face credit risk due to non-payment of interest or principal by the debt/securities issuers or borrowers, especially of bonds or loan services. This should be given special consideration when investing in these markets or loaning out money.

3. Inflation risk

This is the possibility that one's purchasing power could decline with time due to price-level inflation, which consists of rising prices of products and services. If one's investment returns do not outstrip inflation, real-value savings may decrease over time, resulting in diminished real returns from savings accounts, unless inflation risks have been into consideration when one's financial goals were set, retirement strategies planned or investments with inflation-adjusted returns selected.

4. Interest rate risk

This is the potential effect of changes in the interest rates on investments and borrowings, especially on variable-rate loans and fixed-income investments with variable or fixed-term maturity dates or on savings in accounts that bring interest. Interest-rate movements have the power to significantly alter the value of fixed-income investments while at the same time increasing borrowing costs, thus complicating risk management strategies and their potential impact. Understanding the effect of movements in the interest rates on various financial instruments is paramount to successfully mitigating this risk.

5. Longevity risk

Longevity risk refers to the possibility that one may outlive his/her savings and financial resources due to increasing life expectancy. Individuals need to plan for longer retirement periods by making investments that will provide them with a sustainable income throughout their lives. Annuities, pension plans or retirement savings vehicles can help minimize this risk.

6. Liquidity risk

This refers to investments or assets that cannot be quickly liquidated without significant loss of value when immediate funds are required. To mitigate this risk, individuals must maintain an emergency fund and also take into consideration how liquid each of their investments is.

7. Concentration risk

This refers to the risk arising from investing a large proportion of one's funds in one asset or sector and putting too much focus on it, as opposed to diversifying one's investments broadly across assets or sectors. When the concentration of investments happens, a large proportion of the funds in one's portfolio will be exposed to the performance of that sector or asset in which the investment is concentrated.

8. Personal and liability risks

Unpredictable events with financial consequences, such as accidents, disability claims, lawsuits or property damage, fall within this realm of personal and liability risk. Adequate insurance policies, such as health, disability or liability coverage, can help alleviate some of these financial impacts. So, understanding one's insurance needs as well as making sure that one is sufficiently covered is vital when it comes to tackling personal and liability risks.

9. Tax risk

This is the potential adverse impact that changes in the tax laws or regulations could have on an individual's financial position. Tax rates, exemptions, deductions and planning strategies have significant ramifications when it comes to one's tax liabilities. Staying up-to-date on tax regulations with the help of professional advice and creating efficient planning strategies to cope with them may help one manage tax risk more efficiently.

Conclusion

Financial planning for individuals involves the consideration of all risks to their financial well-being, such as market, inflation, interest rate, longevity, liquidity, personal liability and tax risks. Creating an in-depth financial plan with risk mitigation techniques, such as diversification, insurance coverage and long-term investment approaches, will allow individuals to better navigate such threats with confidence while moving closer towards their financial goals with some certainty. Regular reviews should be done so as to accommodate the changing conditions while mitigating the potential threats that arise along the way.

Overview of contingency risk

Contingency risk (also referred to as unexpected or unforeseen risk) is the possibility of events or circumstances that are difficult or impossible to anticipate and can have an outsize influence on an individual's finances. Contingency risks come in different forms and one must always be adequately prepared for them. Here is an overview of the contingency risks in individual financial planning:

1. Job loss or income disruption

One of the primary contingency risks is job loss or income disruption resulting from economic downturns, company restructuring, technological advancements or personal reasons. An unexpected reduction in one's income can seriously disrupt one's financial plans and make it increasingly challenging to meet one's obligations. An emergency fund that covers at least six months' living expenses can provide the necessary financial cushion during job transitions and provide protection.

2. Medical emergencies

Emergencies involving one's health can have serious financial ramifications. In India, where healthcare costs continue to skyrocket, unexpected expenses can quickly exceed budgeted amounts and strain one's finances further. Adequate health insurance, including critical-illness cover, can ease some of this financial strain. However, regular reviews must take place to make sure the policies provide ample protection in case an unexpected contingency arises.

3. Natural disasters and property damage

Natural disasters like floods, earthquakes or cyclones can create immense property damage and financial loss in their wake. Without adequate insurance coverage in place to repair homes and replace belongings that are destroyed in such calamities, individuals could incur high expenses on repair and reconstruction work that may need to be done. Homeowner or renter's insurance policies provide essential protection in these instances.

4. Legal and liability risks

Legal issues or liability claims that may arise unexpectedly can create large financial liabilities. Litigations, lawsuits or personal liability claims could entail costly legal fees or settlement awards for personal injuries sustained through no fault of one's own. Appropriate personal or professional liability policies can provide one financial security against unexpected legal events.

5. Family or personal emergencies

Setbacks or emergencies such as divorce, loss of a loved one or unexpected caregiving responsibilities can cause great disruption to one's finances and create additional expenses, loss of income or changes to one's financial responsibilities that need to be managed effectively. Keeping an up-to-date financial plan that addresses potential contingencies, as well as sufficient insurance, can guide individuals through such situations more smoothly.

6. Economic and political risks

Financial downturns, changes in government policies or political instability can negatively impact both financial markets and individual plans, leading to job loss, reduced returns on investments or currency fluctuations. Diversifying one's investments while keeping oneself up to date with the economic and political developments and being open-minded and informed can help one cope during such events.

Contingency risks are inherent to personal financial planning and must be effectively addressed for your finances to remain stable. Employment loss, medical emergencies, natural disasters, legal and liability risks, family emergencies or personal emergencies, economic risks or political risks are just some of the contingencies individuals may end up having to deal with. Individuals can prepare themselves financially for unanticipated events by creating emergency funds, maintaining appropriate insurance coverage, diversifying their investments and regularly reviewing and revising their financial plans. By taking into consideration the potential contingency risks and employing risk mitigation techniques, they can increase their resilience during times of disruption to their well-being.

Risk-reward trade-off

Financial planning requires individuals to find an equilibrium between risk and reward in accordance with their financial goals, time horizons and risk profiles. There is often a trade-off between higher rewards and increased risks. Therefore, understanding one's risk tolerance and investment objectives is integral to finding an optimal risk-reward balance when it comes to investment. Some prioritize capital preservation over obtaining higher returns and growth, while others pursue more aggressive approaches, seeking greater returns and growth opportunities.

Here are some ways to effectively manage one's risk/reward trade-off:

1. Diversification

This is an investment strategy that involves the dispersal of investments across asset classes, sectors and geographic regions for risk mitigation. By diversifying their investments, individuals can reduce their exposure to specific risks while potentially increasing the reward-to-risk ratio of their portfolio, thus lessening any impact from one investment's poor performance on the overall performance of the portfolio.

2. Asset allocation

Financial planning often begins with identifying the risks in your various choices of investment, evaluating their potential impact and devising a strategy to offset those risks. Asset allocation plays a vital role in risk management, as funds are set aside for various asset classes based on the investor's risk profile and goals. Asset allocation strategies should take into account the investor's acceptable levels of risk diversification potential and the desired reward potential.

3. Time horizon and risk capacity

The time horizon an individual has in mind for his or her investment, or the expected duration for which one expects to remain invested in something, also impacts risk-reward trade-off decisions. Longer time frames allow for greater tolerance of short-term market fluctuations as well as greater capacity for taking on risk; younger investors with longer investment horizons can allocate a larger proportion of their portfolio for growth-oriented investments that can bring potentially higher returns than other types of investment but also have potentially higher volatility; individuals nearing retirement or with shortening time horizons may prefer to take a more conservative route so as to secure the wealth they have accumulated.

4. Reviewing and monitoring

Financial planning should be seen as an ongoing process requiring ongoing reviews and monitoring, especially as market conditions and one's financial goals and risk tolerance may change over time. Regular reassessment of investments allows individuals to ensure that their risk profile remains aligned with their objectives and risk-tolerance levels while making adjustments as needed to arrive at an optimal risk-reward ratio.

Consulting a financial adviser may bring additional assistance in understanding this aspect of finance planning.

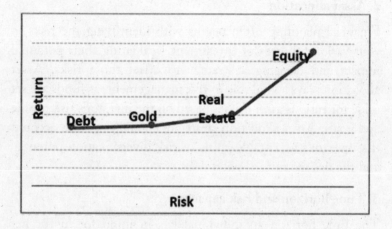

The figure summarized the risk-reward relationship for the most common asset classes. As discussed earlier, 'debt' instruments have the lowest relative return as well as a lower relative risk while higher returns of 'equity' instruments come with higher 'risk'.

Overview of risk profiling

Risk profiling is an essential step in financial planning. It involves the assessment of an individual's risk tolerance and the selection of a suitable investment strategy. An understanding of their own risk profile can help individuals align their investment decisions with their comfort levels, financial goals and time horizons. Furthermore, such an understanding also facilitates the creation of a well-diversified portfolio and effective management of risks. Regular review of one's risk profile as circumstances evolve is highly advised so as to make sure one's investment decisions remain aligned with one's risk tolerance and financial goals.

Here's an overview of the different risk profiles frequently utilized in financial planning:

1. Conservative

Investors with a conservative risk profile prioritize capital preservation and generally shun investments that involve significant fluctuations. They typically opt for safer options like fixed deposits, government bonds or conservative mutual funds in order to generate stable but modest returns while protecting their capital and keeping their investments secure. These investors usually accept lower returns in return for greater safety and stability.

2. Moderate

Investors who possess a moderate risk profile strive for a balance between growth and preservation of capital. They accept some degree of investment volatility in exchange for higher potential returns, allocating part of their portfolio towards relatively stable investments such as bonds or blue-chip stocks while considering growth-oriented funds like diversified equity funds for high returns. Investors with a moderate risk profile aim for optimal levels of growth while mitigating their risks.

3. Balanced

Investors with a balanced risk profile have intermediate risk tolerance and tend to favour an amalgam of conservative and growth investments, accepting some short-term volatility in pursuit of long-term gains. They prefer portfolios consisting of stocks, bonds and other asset classes to achieve steady growth while mitigating risks through diversification.

4. Growth

Investors who fall under this profile typically possess higher risk tolerance than the previous two types and prioritize long-term capital appreciation over short-term market fluctuations and returns. Growth-oriented investors usually allocate a larger portion of their portfolio to stocks or equity-based mutual funds and are in pursuit of long-term gains rather than reacting quickly to short-term market fluctuations.

5. Aggressive

Investors with an aggressive risk profile have extremely high risk tolerance and accept significant investment volatility with ease, prioritizing long-term returns while accepting short-term fluctuations as necessary for the pursuit of their long-term goals. They hold more than 70 per cent of their assets in equity with exposure to high-risk-high-reward segments like small cap and emerging market stocks.

Risk profiles are inherently subjective and dependent on one's personal circumstances, financial goals and investment expertise. Risk profiling allows both investors and advisers to find investment strategies that fit their individual risk tolerance, time horizon and objectives. Regular review of one's risk profile will ensure that it remains reflective of one's evolving circumstances and goals.

Risk assessment

Assessment of one's risk profile is an integral step in financial planning as it helps identify an investment strategy tailored specifically for one, based on one's tolerance level and financial goals. An understanding of an individual's personal risk profile allows financial planners to create balanced plans with balanced risk/reward profiles for that person. Here are some methods and factors one should keep in mind when conducting this assessment:

1. Risk tolerance questionnaires

Financial advisers often utilize risk tolerance questionnaires to assess an individual's investment profile. Usually composed of several questions designed to measure one's comfort with investment risk, this assessment tool may ask for inputs like an individual's time horizon, goals, past investment experiences or reactions to hypothetical market scenarios. The answers will help determine whether an investor is conservative, moderate, balanced or aggressive when it comes to risk. Financial advisers then can recommend the individual appropriate investment options or asset allocation strategies based on these results.

2. Investment knowledge and experience

An individual's knowledge and experience in the matter of investments can play a crucial role in their risk profile assessment. Those with a more in-depth understanding of various investment options, asset classes and market dynamics may feel more at ease with higher-risk investments as they possess both the knowledge and confidence to assess and manage them effectively, whereas individuals who lack extensive investment knowledge might opt for safer or less volatile options instead.

3. Financial goals and time horizon

An individual's financial goals and time horizon for investment should play an integral part in defining his or her risk profile. Short-term goals, like saving for a down payment on a house or for meeting certain financial obligations, will require a more conservative approach in order to protect one's capital, while more long-term objectives, such as retirement planning, may allow for taking on greater risks for higher potential returns.

4. Income and cash-flow stability

Assessment of an individual's income stability and cash flow is vital to understanding his or her risk profile. People with regular and steady employment, like salaried employees, may feel more at ease taking higher investment risks as their steady income can function as a cushion against potential investment losses. On the other hand, people whose income fluctuates frequently, such as self-employed professionals or freelancers, may take more precautionary steps, such as prioritizing capital preservation over liquidity management to manage cash-flow fluctuations effectively.

5. Emotional and psychological factors

Emotional and psychological factors should also be taken into consideration when evaluating people's risk profile. Some have an above-average tolerance for investment volatility and are less likely to be emotionally affected by market fluctuations; these individuals tend to take calculated risks without succumbing to emotional impulses during market upheavals. Others may experience anxiety or stress when the markets are volatile and have to be fit into more conservative risk profiles, in line with their comfort levels. Emotional volatility could impact one's ability to remain invested through market downturns and adhere to one's long-term investment strategy. It may hinder one from staying invested as planned!

6. Consulting with a financial adviser

Guidance from an expert financial adviser can be invaluable when attempting to assess one's individual risk profile. Financial advisers specialize in evaluating risk tolerance and providing personalized recommendations, based on their client's current financial situation, goals and preferences, to create an optimal investment profile and strategy for them. A qualified adviser will explain the potential risks and rewards associated with various investment options while informing individuals of the trade-offs involved in aligning their risk profile with their long-term financial goals.

Risk profiling is not a process done just once and for all. Rather, individuals should revisit their risk profile periodically as their circumstances, goals and risk tolerance can evolve over time. Life events like marriage, birth of children, career changes or retirement can profoundly alter an individual's risk profile.

By understanding their risk tolerance and taking it into account in their financial plan, individuals can strike an equilibrium between their financial goals and risk tolerance and strive towards long-term financial success.

Sample Risk Profile Questionnaire

These nine questions can be used to quickly assess an investor's risk profile.

The scoring for the questionnaire is as below:

- Option a): Assign score of 1
- Option b): Assign score of 2
- Option c): Assign score of 3
- Option d): Assign score of 4
- Option e): Assign score of 5
- Option f): Assign score of 6

After answering the questions and scoring them, sum up the scores of all the questions. The range of the score will be from 9 to 54. The risk assessment based on the score can be as below:

#	Risk Profile	Score Range
1	Conservative	9–17
2	Moderate	18–26
3	Balanced	27–35
4	Growth	36–44
5	Aggressive	45–54

	a)	b)	c)	d)	e)	f)
Q1	**Your age**					
	a) > 60	b) 51–60	c) 41–50	d) 31–40	e) 25–30	f) < 25
Q2	**What is your ideal time horizon for investment?**					
	a) < 1 year	b) 1 to 2 years	c) 2 to 4 years	d) 4 to 6 years	e) 6 to 8 years	f) > 8 years
Q3	**What percentage of your monthly income can you save?**					
	a) < 5%	b) 5 to 10%	c) 11 to 15%	d) 16 to 20%	e) 21 to 25%	f) > 25%
Q4	**Where do most of your investments lie?**					
	a) Fixed Deposits	b) Bonds or Debt MF	c) Equity MF	d) Shares	e) PMS	f) Alternate Assets
Q5	**What returns do you expect from your investments?**					
	a) About 7%	b) 7–10%	c) 11–15%	d) 16–20%	e) 21–25%	f) > 25%
Q6	**What will you do if your investments in equity are down 10%?**					
	a) Never invest in equity again	b) Sell and move money to FDs	c) Sell 50% and hold 50%	d) Do nothing	e) Buy 10% more equity	f) Buy 20% more equity

Q7	How much time will you give an investment to show performance?					
	a) < 3 months	b) 3–6 months	c) 6–12 months	d) 1–2 years	e) 2–3 years	f) > 3 years
Q8	What is your main purpose in investing?					
	a) Highest capital appreciation possible	b) High capital appreciation	c) Medium capital appreciation	d) Regular income with capital appreciation	e) Regular income	f) Protection of capital
Q9	How much loss or risk can you tolerate?					
	a) 31–40%	b) 21–30%	c) 11–20%	d) 5–10%	e) 1–5%	f) Zero

Case study: Rajesh Jhawar—Risk Profiling

Background

Rajesh Jhawar is a forty-five-year-old software engineer working with a reputed IT firm in Kolkata. His annual income is Rs 18 lakh, and he is married with two children, living in a family-owned house in Kolkata. His current investments are in Indian equities, mutual funds, a few government bonds and fixed deposits in nationalized banks.

Objectives

Short-term: Funding children's higher education in India or abroad in five to seven years
Long-term: Retirement planning with a goal to retire by the age of sixty

Financial Review Process

1. Understanding Risk Tolerance

- Conducted through detailed discussions and risk assessment questionnaires
- Rajesh is moderately risk-averse, preferring a balanced approach to investments

2. Assessing Current Financial Position

- Review of assets (including property and investments), liabilities (such as any loans), income and expenses
- Analysis of the liquidity and performance of his current investments

3. Risk Capacity Evaluation

- Factors like age, job security in the IT sector and family commitments are considered

- Assessment of the impact of market volatility on his financial goals

4. Risk Exposure Analysis

- Review of the current investment portfolio to identify overexposure to certain asset classes
- Evaluation of the balance between Indian equities, mutual funds and safer debt instruments

5. Impact of Life Changes

- Consideration of potential life events, including changes in the IT industry, health concerns, or family needs

6. Risk Mitigation Strategies

- Portfolio diversification to include a mix of equities, bonds and fixed-income instruments
- Recommendations for health and life insurance to safeguard against unforeseen circumstances
- Suggestion to create an emergency fund equivalent to six to twelve months of expenses

Conclusion

Rajesh Jhawar's risk profile is **moderately conservative**, in line with many middle-aged professionals in India. His preference for balanced growth and security aligns with his immediate goal of education planning and a stable retirement. A diversified investment strategy is recommended, with periodic rebalancing to align with changing market conditions and personal circumstances.

Key takeaways from this section

1. Assess your total annual income from all sources
2. Assess your total annual expenses
3. Analyse your net cash flow, which is your total annual income minus your total annual expenses
4. Set aside the amount you will save from your net cash flow
5. A good savings ratio will be about 20 per cent of your annual income
6. Assess your total assets, both financial and physical
7. Assess your total liabilities, both short term and long term
8. Know your net worth. The net worth is the difference between total assets and total liabilities
9. Savings and net worth are critical inputs for the creation of a financial plan
10. Assess your risk profile

Section 2: Create a Plan (C)

'The best way to predict your future is to create it.'
—Peter Drucker

After assessing your current financial situation, the next step is to create a plan that will help you achieve your financial goals. This involves setting specific, measurable, achievable, relevant and time-bound (SMART) goals. Your plan should include the ranking of your goals, optimal asset allocation and strategies for reducing debt and increasing savings. It is important to revisit your plan regularly and make adjustments as needed.

Chapter 4

Goal-Setting

Financial planning is a systematic approach to using money wisely so as to achieve your life goals. The process includes an in-depth examination of your current financial status, the setting and prioritization of goals, the formulation of an action plan to reach these objectives, regular review of your progress towards this plan on an ongoing basis and then updating your plan as necessary. Timelines play an integral part in financial planning, as they dictate what investment options are available, your risk tolerance levels and your overall strategic decisions.

Understanding your financial situation

At the foundation of financial planning lies your understanding of your current financial status—knowledge of your income, expenses, assets, liabilities, risk tolerance, etc., as described earlier.

Now that you understand your financial status and have a clear picture of your life goal, aligning with your financial goals should become part of your daily routine. To create an efficient personal finance goal-setting process, follow these steps.

1. Evaluate your financial situation

Evaluate the details of your monthly income and expenses by factoring in all sources (salary, rental income, etc.) against all expenses such as rent, groceries and transportation. Additionally, consider your assets (real estate, stocks, mutual funds, etc.) against your liabilities (home loan, personal loan, credit card debt, etc.). You can calculate your net worth from this, as described earlier.

2. Establish your financial goals

Reflect upon what financial milestones you wish to reach—for example, purchase of a home, saving for college tuition expenses for your children, planning an efficient retirement portfolio or an overseas trip.

3. Establish SMART financial goals

Your goals should be specific, measurable, achievable, relevant and time-bound to help ensure they will actually happen. Rather than setting generic retirement savings goals, such as 'I want to save for retirement,' make your goals specific—for example, 'I plan to save Rs 2 crore by age sixty.'

4. Categorize your goals based on your time horizon for them

Classify your goals based on their expected dates of achievement to more efficiently allocate and prioritize resources towards meeting all your financial objectives. This exercise helps set clearer priorities when prioritizing finances for long-term objectives.

5. Prioritize your goals

Ranking your goals from 'P1' to 'Pn' is the easiest and simplest way to identify which ones are of highest priority to you, P1 being given top billing and Pn receiving no consideration at all. Establishing your priorities allows you to direct your effort, time and financial resources towards those goals which align best with your values and aspirations. Making more informed decisions regarding where your income, savings and investments go can also ensure that progress is being made towards your more important financial objectives.

6. Estimate the savings needs for each goal

Estimating the total investments required on your part for each of your goals and breaking up those investments into manageable savings targets require the consideration of factors like the time horizons you have in mind, the inflation rates and any associated costs. Using those figures, you can then set realistic savings goals for the allocation of funds for each of your objectives.

7. Allocate savings and assets according to priority

This involves matching up financial resources with each goal's importance and time horizon. Prioritized goals, such as emergency funds or near-term objectives, often necessitate more conservative savings instruments, like savings accounts or short-term deposits. Medium-term goals could benefit from an array of savings and moderate-risk investments; long-term ones may require higher-risk vehicles like stocks or mutual funds to drive potential growth. By pairing savings and investment instruments with each goal, you can optimize your financial resources while increasing the probability of their fulfilment. Furthermore, this exercise will also assist with identifying low-priority goals which need to be abandoned or postponed.

8. Establish a budget

A budget involves making a careful inventory of both your income and expenditure in order to craft an account that aligns with your financial goals, tracks your spending habits and savings, where applicable, and also allocates your savings to investments related to those goals. A good budget enables you to prioritize your financial goals while controlling your spending habits so as to stay within your means. The purpose of the budget is to ensure financial stability and prosperity for years to come.

9. Monitor your progress

Regularly assess your financial health using online tools or apps which sync up with your bank accounts to get an accurate picture of where you stand.

10. Review and alter your goals

As life circumstances shift, so must your goals. Marriage, children, health issues, job changes or income adjustments all may necessitate modifications to your financial goals.

Financial planning should not be seen as a one-time activity. It is an ongoing journey. Your plan must adapt to your life changes and the shifts in your financial situation. Seeking advice from financial advisers may also prove helpful.

Goal-setting with the SMART Framework

The SMART framework can be effectively utilized when setting financial management goals. SMART, as we have said before, stands for specific, measurable, achievable, relevant and time-bound. Here we elaborate on each of these qualities.

1. Specific

One key part of setting financial goals is to make sure they are defined and specific. Broad or vague goals, like 'I want to save money' or 'I want to become wealthy', do not provide an efficient road map for success. Vagueness will make it hard for you to identify which steps or actions need to be taken towards attaining your goal.

Consider someone who says, 'I want to save money.' While this statement expresses a laudable intention, its lack of specificity leaves numerous unanswered questions: For what purpose is that person saving money? How much money must be saved and within what time frame?

Establish clear financial goals instead—for example, 'I want to save Rs 10 lakh in ten years' time for my child's education.' Specific goals help focus your efforts and increase your motivation. Knowing exactly where your efforts are leading to is more rewarding!

2. Measurable

All financial goals should be measurable, in that you must be able to track their progress towards completion and know when you have reached them. Otherwise, it will be impossible to ascertain whether any progress towards your goals is being made or whether any adjustments in your plan are required.

Imagine setting a ten-year goal of saving Rs 10 lakh for your child's education. Here, a specific sum of Rs 10 lakh needs to be saved. Keeping track of your monthly or annual savings will help you monitor your progress towards this goal. Once Rs 5 lakh has been saved in five years, you know you are halfway to meeting your target!

Setting a measurable goal not only allows you to track your progress and stay on target in your saving or investment habits, but it can also keep your motivation high and keep growing your savings over time. Witnessing your savings rise is enough motivation for most.

3. Achievable

Setting financial goals that are ambitious but also realistic will increase your chances of achieving them successfully and decrease the possibility that you might feel discouraged or give up altogether.

If you earn Rs 50,000 monthly and your expenses total Rs 45,000 each month, then your savings will be Rs 5000 each month. An ambitious savings goal of Rs 20 lakh in ten years is likely not achievable. An attainable target might be savings of Rs 10.52 lakh in ten years, by starting an SIP of Rs 5000 (assuming an effective interest rate of 12 per cent p.a.). You will have to find ways to cut your expenses or boost your income to increase your monthly savings to Rs 9500 (assuming the same interest rate of 12 per cent) in order to achieve Rs 20 lakh in ten years.

To set realistic financial goals, it is necessary to assess your current situation carefully. Consider all your income, expenses and any financial commitments, as this information will help you determine which goals of yours can be accomplished or are within reach.

4. Relevant

Your financial goals must reflect your life circumstances, values and long-term ambitions for maximum motivation and commitment on your part. If they are not relevant, financial goals become much harder to set.

In terms of setting short-term goals that relate to the attainment of long-term objectives such as early retirement, it might not make sense to set a short-term goal of purchasing an expensive car. Instead, a more relevant goal would be to invest a fixed amount from your salary each month towards building up your retirement fund.

Your financial goals must align with your overall life plan. If you need help in understanding what long-term goals to set, financial planning may be worth exploring. This involves taking an in-depth look at your own life and at the financial industry to establish what long-term goals can be pursued.

5. Time-bound

Every financial goal needs a deadline, otherwise it risks becoming simply another dream that's never realized. Without deadlines, you may not make steady progress towards your goal, and your neglect of it may make it a pressing need and an obligation.

When you set your financial goals, consider when you want them achieved. For instance, saving for higher education for your child, who is currently five years old, may mean saving Rs 10 lakh in thirteen years' time.

Setting a time frame for your goals will provide you with a framework to work with. Additionally, setting an exact date for your goals will allow you to plan your savings or investments accordingly. For instance, if your goals are long-term ones, they will involve investment in equities or mutual funds, which typically offer greater returns over a long time frame; otherwise, you will have to invest in fixed deposits which will offer capital protection.

Apply SMART goals

There are many tools and products in the Indian financial landscape that can assist you in achieving your SMART financial goals and tailor options for you specifically towards meeting your individual goals, your risk tolerance levels and your investment timelines. An understanding of the available solutions allows for the selection of those most suited to meet your particular requirements.

For retirement savings in India, two excellent long-term investment vehicles are the National Pension System (NPS) and the Public Provident Fund (PPF). Each of them offers tax breaks while being government-backed, offering relative safety.

If you are saving for education expenses or the down payment on a home, an ideal savings vehicle would be a recurring deposit or a high-interest fixed deposit (FD). Both products provide safe returns guaranteed monthly or yearly, enabling you to save regular amounts each month or year.

If you're willing to accept higher risk in exchange for potentially higher returns, investing in stocks or mutual funds could be worth exploring. The equity-linked savings scheme (ELSS) is one type of mutual fund that offers both high potential returns as well as tax savings benefits.

Investment in the stock market entails risks that must be understood and accepted. Make sure you seek guidance from an adviser or conduct extensive research before diving in!

Setting SMART financial goals is critical to financial success. They will offer you a clear road map and make your journey towards realizing your goals much simpler. There are several tools available in India to assist you in this goal-setting. Take some time to explore them and select those that best align with your objectives.

Case study: Ravi Gowda—Goal of Buying a House[*]

Background

Ravi Gowda, twenty-eight, is a software engineer living in Bengaluru. He earns a salary of Rs 2 lakh a month. His monthly expenses amount to Rs 60,000. He lives in a rented apartment. His dream is to own a house in the city. Ravi realizes that he must set financial goals to make that goal come true.

Ravi's SMART goals

Specific

Ravi decides he wants to purchase a two-bedroom apartment in one of Bengaluru's prime localities for Rs 80 lakh and will save enough for the 20 per cent down payment (Rs 16 lakh) as soon as possible.

---

[*] To keep the case study simple, inflation on house price and interest on monthly savings are assumed as zero.

Measurable

Ravi has set himself a quantifiable goal of saving Rs 16 lakh. This will allow him to monitor his progress and know when he has accomplished it.

Achievable

In order to meet his goal, Ravi must assess his capacity for saving money. After accounting for expenses, he estimates that he can comfortably set aside Rs 40,000 each month. This would amount to annual savings of approximately Rs 4,80,000!

Relevant

Ravi considers the purchase of a flat an important goal. Owning one would bring him financial security as well as meet his long-term plan to start a family.

Time-bound

Given his savings capacity of approximately Rs 4.8 lakh per annum, Ravi sets himself a time limit of roughly three and a half years to meet his savings goal of Rs 16 lakh.

Ravi sets his savings goal with this approach in mind and decides to place his savings in both high-interest fixed deposits (FDs) and mutual funds, both offering safe yet guaranteed returns, the mutual funds offering potentially higher returns at greater risk. He also decides to increase the amount of his savings with each salary raise. In doing this, he now has laid out a clear road map towards purchasing his dream house. He knows exactly how much needs to be saved, for how long and what steps he needs to take.

Categorize goals based on timelines

You can have short-term, medium-term and long-term goals, depending on the time horizon you have in mind.

Short-term financial goals

Your short-term financial goals should be achievable within three years and will require your immediate focus. They often serve as steps towards meeting your longer-term targets. Common examples of such short-term targets would be the building of an emergency fund, clearing of credit card debts or saving for a vacation.

Short-term goals typically entail less risk compared with long-term ones because they tend to rely more on savings than on investments. In India, savings accounts, short-term fixed deposits, liquid mutual funds or arbitrage mutual funds may be suitable investment instruments in this regard, as they will provide you easy access to your money, which is vital when meeting short-term goals.

Attainment of short-term goals calls for regular savings and careful budgeting. Knowing how much can realistically be saved each month and sticking with that plan are the key points to keep in mind when working towards them. Furthermore, keeping your short-term savings separate from the money you use for everyday spends will reduce the temptation on your part to dip into them for uses other than saving.

Medium-term goals

Medium-term financial goals are those you hope to meet within three to seven years. They are the intermediate goals that lie between your short- and long-term goals. Some common medium-term objectives would be saving for a down payment on a house, saving to buy a car or to fund your child's primary education.

Due to their longer time frames, medium-term goals allow for more risk-taking. Balanced funds or hybrid funds that invest in both equity and debt investments could be suitable options in India for meeting such targets—they aim to balance risk against returns over a medium time span.

To meet medium-term goals, you need a specific plan and disciplined execution. Establish how much money must be saved each month or each year until your target has been attained and stick with that commitment.

Long-term financial goals

Your long-term financial goals should involve the attainment of significant savings and investments over more than seven years. They may have to do with the major milestones of life, such as retirement, buying a house, higher education or your child's marriage.

Longer time frames allow investors to take on more risk as there's ample opportunity to recover from any short-term losses. Therefore, the suitable instruments for such investments would be equity mutual funds or NPS investments. Equity exposure provides higher long-term returns even if they sometimes experience short-term volatility.

Long-term goals require consistent saving and investing over an extended period of time. Starting early gives your funds more time to grow through the compounding of interest, while your risk appetite might shift, depending on when and what goal is neared. For instance, as retirement approaches, you might wish to switch your portfolio away from high-risk instruments like equity to safer options like bonds in order to preserve capital. Such strategies as 'lifecycle investing' help mitigate risk over time as your time horizon changes.

Case study: Pavan Rao—Setting Financial Goals

Background

Pavan Rao is an IT professional residing in Hyderabad, earning a monthly salary of Rs 1.5 lakh. He has set several financial goals for himself.

1. *Short-term goal (1–3 years):* Pavan plans on purchasing a car worth Rs 9 lakh within three years, which requires

him to save approximately Rs 23,500 monthly. In order to meet this short-term goal, he decides to invest his savings in an attractive low-risk recurring deposit (RD) scheme. His invested value of Rs 8.64 lakh will be worth Rs 9.02 lakh at the end of three years, assuming a 6.5 per cent effective interest rate.

2. *Medium-term goal (3–7 years):* Pavan has a ten-year-old daughter who will go to university in seven years' time. Pavan wishes to save Rs 20 lakh for her higher studies at university. Given its long-term nature, this goal calls for long-term investment strategies with an effective annual return of around 14 per cent. An approximate monthly investment of Rs 15,600 would have to be made for this target.

3. *Long-term goal (7+ years):* Pavan plans on retiring at sixty with a corpus of about Rs 3 crore. He has twenty-five years left to save this amount. He decides to invest his savings through a systematic investment plan (SIP) in diversified equity mutual funds with an expected effective return of 13 per cent per annum. To meet his target, he needs to save approximately Rs 16,100 each month until retirement day arrives.

Pavan maintains a portfolio of investments across various time horizons and risks to ensure there is diversity and his financial plans are on course. Every year he reviews his financial goals and investment performance to make sure he's still on track and adjusts or switches investments as necessary.

This example is a simplified one. Real-world factors, including inflation, changes in one's income or unexpected expenses, as well as market fluctuations, may call for further adjustments in your plan and may necessitate consulting a financial adviser for personalized guidance and advice.

Once you understand and differentiate between needs and desires, categorizing your goals becomes much simpler. They should then be divided into low-, medium- and high-priority ones for easy review.

High-priority goals

These goals should focus on what is essential for your financial security and well-being. They would include:

The emergency fund

Every household should establish an emergency fund as an insurance policy against unexpected events like a job loss or expenses such as medical costs.

Repayment of high-interest debts

Debts such as credit card dues can drain your income because of the high interest rates charged, making their repayment an immediate priority.

Retirement savings

Starting early can make all the difference; compound interest will do its work and quickly grow your nest egg! Don't put off starting your retirement savings. Start today to ensure yourself a secure future! A monthly SIP of Rs 16,000 invested over thirty years will generate a corpus of Rs 5.64 crore; the corpus drops to Rs 1.60 crore if the investment horizon falls to twenty years (assuming an expected annual return of 12 per cent).

Medium-priority goals

These objectives should be seen as important but less pressing than the high-priority goals. Some examples of medium-priority goals could be:

Buying a home

Home ownership can be an enormously costly financial goal for many, but once your emergency fund and high-interest debts have been dealt with, saving for a home can become your focus. Once this goal has been established, start setting money aside as savings towards your dream home purchase!

Investing for wealth creation

Once your high-priority goals have been accomplished, investing can become another avenue towards wealth creation, whether as part of your medium-term goals or your general wealth accumulation plans.

Children's education

If you have children, saving for their education should be one of your higher-priority goals. As costs associated with higher education continue to escalate rapidly, saving early could make all the difference!

Low-priority goals

These should aim to enrich your lifestyle but aren't essential to your financial security. They would typically include things or indulgences such as:

Vacations and luxury purchases

Vacations, luxury purchases and hobbies fall into this category and should only come after your high- and medium-priority goals have been accomplished.

Donations to charity

If philanthropy is important to you, you can provide for charitable donations in your financial plan. This should come after first securing yourself financially.

Prioritization of your financial goals can be an arduous and individualistic task. It should reflect your unique circumstances, values and future aspirations. To start the process properly, understand your goals by differentiating between needs and desires, categorizing each as low, medium and high priority before reviewing and revising them regularly.

Striking a balance between short-term and long-term goals

Prioritization of goals calls for striking a delicate balance between long-term objectives, like saving for retirement or purchasing a house; and medium- or low-priority goals (saving for a vacation, etc.). For optimal financial health, it's vital that resources be distributed equally between short-term goals and long-term ones.

Risk evaluation and administration

One often overlooked aspect of financial planning is risk. Every goal carries some degree of risk; understanding your risk tolerance and using that to arrive at goal prioritization for yourself will ensure that you're happy with the steps being taken towards meeting your goals. For instance, investing in the stock market carries the possibility of big returns but also risk. Saving money in bank accounts entails lower risk but also fetches lower returns.

Align goals with values

Your financial goals should reflect both your values and life aspirations. For instance, if environmental sustainability is important to you, investing in sustainable companies or purchasing a house with low carbon emissions would be your top goals. Or perhaps family is at the top of your priority list, and saving for their education or buying a larger property is a high-priority goal for you. By aligning your goals with your values, you can ensure that your plan supports you in living the life you envision for yourself.

Establishing goals and the savings needed to reach them are central to financial planning.

Case study: Kavita Mishra—Establishing Goals and Savings Needs

Background

Let's use Kavita Mishra, a thirty-year-old marketing manager living in Delhi, as an example to demonstrate this process.

Step 1: Identification of financial goals

Kavita begins by identifying her short-term, medium-term and long-term financial goals.

- *Short-term goal (1–3 years):* Purchase of a car costing Rs 8 lakh in two years
- *Medium-term goal (3–7 years):* Pursuit of an MBA programme at a top-tier institution, which she estimates will cost about Rs 20 lakh at today's value five years later
- *Long-term goal (7+ years):* Savings of Rs 2 crore by the time of her retirement at age sixty

Step 2: Inflation adjustment

Next, Kavita adjusts these goals for inflation since the cost of her goals will rise over time. Assuming an average inflation rate of 5 per cent per annum, her goals become:

- *Car:* Rs 8 lakh * $(1.05)^2$ = Rs 8.82 lakh
- *MBA:* Rs 20 lakh * $(1.05)^5$ = Rs 25.52 lakh
- *Retirement:* Assuming her retirement is thirty years away and the retirement corpus would need to sustain her for another twenty-five years, computing this gets a bit complex. It is advisable for Kavita to use the retirement calculators available online. The objective for

Kavita is to ensure that her corpus can provide her with a comfortable inflation-adjusted income throughout her retirement years

Step 3: Calculation of monthly savings

Kavita then calculates how much she needs to save each month to achieve these goals. She assumes an average return of 8 per cent per year from her investments. Using a financial calculator or a simple Excel function, she computes the following:

- *Car:* To accumulate Rs 8.82 lakh in two years, she needs to save approximately Rs 35,500 per month
- *MBA:* To accumulate Rs 25.52 lakh in five years, she needs to save around Rs 36,250 per month
- *Retirement:* The exact monthly savings required would depend on various factors, including her expected lifespan, retirement lifestyle, etc. For this purpose, it's best for her to use an online retirement calculator

Step 4: Review and adjustment

Kavita reviews her financial goals and savings plan in order to adapt them to any changes in income, expenses or circumstances that occur, making sure her plan accommodates them as needed.

Step 5: Utilization of financial tools

Kavita uses a financial planning app to monitor her savings and her progress towards her goals while also consulting a professional adviser, as needed, for tailored advice.

Step 6: Saving and investing

Finally, Kavita begins saving and investing according to her plan. To stay on track on this task, she has provided for automatic transfer of funds from her savings accounts to her investment accounts, so as to be compliant with her plan.

As Kavita can see, by setting financial goals, adjusting them for inflation and computing her required monthly savings, she can work towards reaching them. Of course, it should be remembered that this process requires ongoing evaluations and adjustments as it unfolds, so Kavita must remain flexible enough to adjust or change her plans as required to remain on course on her path towards her financial objectives.

Chapter 5

Asset Allocation Strategy

Security-focused asset allocation

Security-focused investing may be best for investors prioritizing safety and stability over high growth, such as those nearing retirement or those who prefer low-risk investments that won't experience large fluctuations.

Security-focused portfolios typically focus on investments that bring fixed-income security, such as bonds, fixed deposits (FD), Public Provident Fund (PPF), National Savings Certificate (NSC), Kisan Vikas Patra (KVP) and Sukanya Samriddhi Yojana (SSY). Bonds and post office schemes (NSC, KVP, SSY) issued by governments tend to offer reduced default risk; fixed deposits at banks provide fixed rates of return over specified time frames and are insured up to a certain limit by the Deposit Insurance and Credit Guarantee Corporation (DICGC).

Blue-chip stocks should represent part of an investor's portfolio as they offer stable returns while not experiencing as much market volatility as the smaller, high-growth company stocks. While their potential returns might not match up exactly with those of the latter, they provide greater security against market swings.

Gold is another asset often included in security-oriented portfolios as it represents a safe-haven investment. Gold holds deep cultural significance for Indians and can serve as an antidote against inflation; you can purchase physical gold, such as jewellery or coins, or invest in gold exchange-traded funds (ETFs) or sovereign gold bonds (SGB).

Real estate is another form of security in an investment portfolio. Property ownership can provide regular rental income streams, and property also tends to appreciate in value over time. However, property acquisition requires significant capital and can be affected by many outside influences and so should be approached very carefully.

An investment strategy focused on security-sensitive investments is aimed at mitigating risk and protecting capital; the returns might not match up with what more aggressive strategies can bring, but there is less risk of one losing it all.

Case study: Rahul Bakshi—Security-Focused Asset Allocation

Background

Rahul Bakshi is nearly sixty years old and close to retirement at work. He is looking for an effective investment plan that is low-risk with an emphasis on capital preservation. Let's look at his allocation.

Dividend-Paying Stocks

Rahul allocates 20 per cent of his portfolio to blue-chip stocks known for consistent dividend payments. Companies in sectors like utilities, pharmaceuticals and consumer goods are often considered for their stability and dividend history.

Bonds

To add a layer of stability, Rahul invests 40 per cent in a mix of government bonds for security and corporate bonds for potentially higher returns. He carefully balances risk and return based on his risk tolerance and income needs.

Fixed and Recurring Deposits

Rahul decides to keep 30 per cent of his portfolio in fixed deposits and recurring deposits offered by reputable banks. These provide him with a steady and predictable interest income at regular intervals.

Gold ETF

Rahul decides to keep 10 per cent of his portfolio in gold ETF to provide him with inflation protection.

In conclusion, Rahul's security-focused investment strategy combines a diversified set of assets to generate a regular stream of income while considering the need for capital preservation in his retirement years.

Income-focused asset allocation

Income-focused strategies are for investors looking for regular returns from their investments. Retirees who require a steady monthly income to cover their living costs often use them. But anyone who possesses significant wealth could also use them.

There are numerous income-generating assets in the Indian capital markets that are worth exploring. Dividend-paying stocks may provide investors with an additional source of dividend income, while capital-growth opportunities abound.

Bonds are an essential element of an income-focused portfolio. By buying bonds, investors effectively lend money directly to the bond issuers in exchange for regular interest payments in return. Government, corporate and tax-free bonds should all be taken into consideration; each offers different risks and returns, so investors should carefully weigh all the available choices when selecting bonds to invest in.

Fixed deposits are other sources of steady income. Offered by banks, these provide interest at fixed rates at regular intervals— for example, monthly, quarterly or yearly—and can be a steady source of funds.

Real estate investments can bring rental payments as a source of regular income, but they require significant upfront capital outlay and ongoing property management responsibilities. But real estate investment trusts (REITs) enable investors to earn rental income without the bother of owning and overseeing properties themselves.

Annuities provided by insurance companies also warrant consideration, providing regular payments in return for an up-front lump-sum payment or for life. Annuities provide investors with security during their retirement years by guaranteeing regular income streams from insurance payments over time.

An income-focused investment strategy seeks to generate regular, sustainable streams of income while protecting the capital. Care must be taken when devising this type of approach to investments.

Case study: Meera Mehta—Income-Focused Retirement Portfolio

Background

Meera Mehta is a sixty-five-year-old retiree looking for steady income from her investments. Let's look at her investment allocation as per her goal.

Dividend-Paying Stocks

Meera has strategically allocated 40 per cent of her financial portfolio to dividend-paying equity shares. These blue-chip stocks, selected from stable sectors like utilities and pharmaceuticals, aim to provide her with a consistent and reliable source of dividend income.

Bonds

To enhance stability in her portfolio, Meera has invested 30 per cent in a mix of government and corporate bonds. This allocation ensures regular interest payments, contributing to her overall income stream. The careful balance between risk and return aligns with her risk tolerance and income requirement.

Fixed Deposits

Meera has allocated 20 per cent of funds in fixed deposits offered by reputable banks. These fixed-rate deposits provide her with a steady and predictable interest income at regular intervals, contributing to the stability of her cash flow.

Real Estate Investment Trusts (REITs)

Meera has allocated the remaining 10 per cent of her portfolio to REITs. This investment avenue allows her to benefit from a rental income without the burden of property management. The diversified nature of REITs aligns with her goal of generating regular income.

In conclusion, Meera's income-focused investment strategy is tailored to her retirement goals, providing a balanced mix of stability and regular income.

Growth-focused asset allocation

Growth-focused asset allocation strategies are best suited for investors willing to accept more risk in exchange for potentially higher returns. They tend to work best in the case of younger investors who can tolerate market fluctuations over longer time frames.

Indian investors considering growth-focused portfolios would do well to invest in stocks, as these have traditionally produced higher long-term returns than other asset classes, though investing in stocks also means taking on greater risk. However, these investors can consider diversification of their stocks by buying blue-chip, mid-cap and small-cap stocks.

Blue-chip stocks, i.e., shares in large, well-established companies, tend to be more stable and have proven records of consistent growth over time, while smaller-cap and mid-cap shares typically offer greater growth potential but may be more volatile.

Investors may also explore sectors with high growth potential. For example, technology has seen significant development over time as digital transformation progresses.

Mutual funds and exchange-traded funds (ETFs) can also provide investors with an effective means of diversification at lower costs than individual stocks or bonds, helping them to decrease their overall risk exposure.

Real estate and commodities are other potential avenues for growth investing, as both can appreciate over time. Real estate can also simultaneously produce rental income, and commodities like gold can serve as an insurance against inflation and market instability.

Investors can also look for growth-oriented fixed-income products like convertible bonds that offer potential for capital appreciation if the underlying company performs strongly.

Case study: Ishan Sharma—Growth-Focused Portfolio

Background

Ishan Sharma, an ambitious thirty-year-old professional, seeks to grow his wealth over time and is open to accepting higher risk in pursuit of higher potential returns. His investment strategy reflects a growth-focused approach, acknowledging the trade-off between risk and potential rewards.

Equity Mutual Funds

Ishan strategically allocates the majority of his funds to equity mutual funds, encompassing large-, mid- and small-cap stocks. This diversified approach aims to capture different levels of growth potential while managing the associated risks.

Real Estate

Recognizing the growth potential in real estate, Ishan allocates 15 per cent of his funds to this asset class. Real estate not only has the potential for appreciation over time but also offers the opportunity for rental income, adding a layer of income to his growth-oriented portfolio.

Gold

Ishan diversifies further by allocating another 15 per cent to gold. This serves as an inflation-protection strategy, as gold historically acts as a hedge against inflation and market instability. The precious metal adds a defensive element to his overall growth-focused portfolio.

In conclusion, Ishan's case study illustrates the effectiveness of a growth-focused portfolio, combining equities with strategic diversification into real estate and gold. This approach aligns with his long-term wealth growth goals while considering the associated risks and potential rewards.

Tax-efficiency-focused asset allocation

Tax-efficiency strategies aim to optimize returns while minimizing their tax impact, which is especially advantageous for individuals in the higher tax brackets. India provides numerous investments with tax benefits.

Equity-linked savings schemes (ELSSs) are popular tax-efficient investments. As mutual funds that invest in a diversified portfolio of stocks, ELSSs allow investors income tax deduction under Section 80C of the Income-tax Act on their investments in them, subject to a limit.

Public Provident Fund (PPF) and National Pension System (NPS) investments are tax-efficient investment instruments, with contributions to them being eligible for deduction under Section 80C, while any interest earned from them is tax-free.

Investors could consider tax-saving fixed deposits, which provide tax deductions up to a certain limit under Section 80C; however, any interest earned on these investments will be taxed as income.

Life and health insurance premiums qualify for tax deductions under Sections 80C and 80D respectively. Your choice of suitable policies could form part of an effective tax-efficient strategy.

Consideration should also be given to the holding period when making investments. In India, long-term capital gains from stocks and equity mutual funds may be tax-free up to certain limits; short-term gains, however, incur higher taxation as compared to long-term capital gains. Therefore, holding investments over an extended period can prove to be more tax-efficient.

Case study: Veer Rana—Tax Efficiency-Focused Portfolio

Background

Veer Rana, in his late forties, desires to maximize his after-tax returns by investing in tax-efficient investment instruments. Recognizing the significance of tax planning, he strategically allocates his investments to take advantage of various tax benefits available in India. Let's look at his investment portfolio.

Equity-Linked Savings Schemes (ELSS)

Veer invests 30 per cent of his portfolio in ELSS funds. These mutual funds not only offer potential returns through equity investments but also provide income tax deductions under Section 80C, enhancing his tax efficiency.

Public Provident Fund (PPF)

Veer allocates 20 per cent of his portfolio in PPF, benefiting from both tax deductions under Section 80C and tax-free interest earned. This tax-efficient fixed-income instrument contributes to his overall tax-efficient strategy.

Term Insurance Plans

Veer allocates 25 per cent of his portfolio in term insurance plans, with premium payments qualifying for tax deductions under both Sections 80C and later 80D for health coverage. This dual benefit adds to the tax efficiency of his portfolio while ensuring financial protection.

Equity Investments

Veer allocates 25 per cent of his investments in long-term equity investments. By strategically maintaining these investments for over a year, Veer aims to benefit from the tax exemptions on long-term capital gains, thereby optimizing the tax impact on his returns.

In conclusion, Veer's case study illustrates the effectiveness of a tax-efficiency-focused portfolio, combining various instruments to optimize after-tax returns while strategically planning for long-term capital gains exemptions.

Balanced asset allocation

Balanced asset allocation strategies seek to achieve an equilibrium between risk and return, offering investors in their mid-career stage or transitioning into retirement the possibility of both income and growth potential.

An Indian balanced portfolio may consist of an eclectic mixture of stocks, bonds and cash investments. It will have both growth assets and investments that bring stability/income.

Diversification is crucial in building a balanced portfolio. This means investments have to be spread across various asset classes and within each asset class too. For instance, an investor with a balanced asset portfolio might hold large-cap, mid-cap and small-cap stocks, both domestic and international, as well as government and corporate bonds of various maturities.

Balanced mutual funds, also referred to as hybrid funds, may be an ideal way of creating an equitable portfolio. These mutual funds invest in both equity and fixed-income securities to offer both growth potential as well as income generation.

Case study: Mina Nair—Balanced Asset Allocation

Background

Mina Nair, a forty-five-year-old corporate employee from Delhi, desires to achieve a balanced approach to her investments, seeking both growth and income. Her investment strategy reflects a cautious yet innovative approach, considering a diverse set of asset classes for equilibrium between risk and return. Let's look at her portfolio allocation.

Equity Mutual Funds

Mina allocates 50 per cent of her portfolio to large-cap, mid-cap and small-cap mutual funds. This diversified equity exposure caters to her growth objective, allowing her to participate in the potential of various market segments.

Bonds

Mina allocates 30 per cent of her portfolio in a mix of government and corporate bonds with different maturities. This fixed-income component provides stability to her portfolio while generating regular income.

Fixed Deposits and Gold ETFs

Mina allocates 20 per cent of her portfolio to fixed deposits and gold ETFs. Fixed deposits offer a steady and predictable source of income, while gold ETFs act as a hedge against market uncertainties, providing diversification.

In conclusion, Mina's case study illustrates the effectiveness of a balanced asset allocation strategy, considering a mix of equities, fixed-income securities and defensive assets to achieve both growth and income objectives.

Aggressive growth-focused asset allocation

Dream or aggressive growth-focused strategies are best suited to investors willing to accept high levels of risk in the hope of getting potentially substantial returns. They are therefore ideal for young investors with long investment horizons and high risk-tolerance levels.

An Indian dream or aggressive growth-focused portfolio might include heavy exposure to equity investments, specifically small-cap and mid-cap stocks with greater growth potential but which also come with greater risks compared with their larger peers. Furthermore, investors could look at sector-specific funds with high growth prospects as part of this approach.

Emerging technologies, including artificial intelligence (AI), fintech and e-commerce, are revolutionizing India's economy, providing companies operating within these fields immense growth opportunities.

Alternative investments, like real estate and commodities, may form part of an aggressive growth-focused portfolio. Although such assets can be more risky and less liquid than their more established counterparts, they also potentially offer greater returns than them too.

Venture capital and private equity represent aggressive investments with potential for high returns. Both involve making stake investments in early-stage or private companies with high-risk profiles but with substantial potential returns.

Finally, it should be remembered that any aggressive growth-focused strategy requires careful management and the willingness to adapt as market conditions alter. Furthermore, diversifying across various assets and sectors will help mitigate the risks involved.

Case study: Arjun Reddy—Aggressive Growth-Focused Portfolio

Background

Arjun Reddy, a twenty-five-year-old tech professional is willing to accept higher risks in order to achieve potentially higher rewards. Let's look at his portfolio allocation.

Small and Mid-Cap Equity Mutual Funds

Arjun allocates 60 per cent of his portfolio to small and mid-cap equity mutual funds. These investments have higher growth potential but come with increased risk compared to larger peers, aligning with his aggressive growth approach.

Sector Funds

Arjun allocates 20 per cent of his portfolio to sector funds, focusing on technology and healthcare. This targeted approach allows him to capitalize on the potential growth within these high-growth industries.

International Equity Funds

Arjun diversifies globally by allocating 10 per cent to international equity funds. This provides him with exposure to international markets, specifically targeting global growth opportunities and adding a layer of diversification to his aggressive portfolio.

Real Estate

Arjun allocates 10 per cent of his portfolio in real estate. While real estate can be less liquid and riskier, it offers the potential for substantial returns and enhances the overall diversification of his aggressive growth-focused portfolio.

In conclusion, Arjun's high-risk tolerance coupled with his long-term investment horizon has prepared him well against market fluctuations.

Chapter 6

Contingency Planning

Contingency planning in finance refers to preparing for unexpected or unanticipated events that could jeopardize your finances in unforeseen or sudden ways, like a job loss, illness or even someone's death. Contingency plans serve to protect both yourself and your loved ones from the consequences of unexpected events that can lead to financial harm. They ensure you a seamless financial future in case of life-altering events or unexpected trouble that may hit hard financially.

Here is how you can prepare for contingencies:

1. Establish an emergency fund

The initial step in contingency planning is to create an emergency fund containing money intended to cover your living expenses for several months should any unanticipated events such as a job loss occur or unexpected expenses arise.

2. Take the necessary insurance policies

As part of your contingency planning strategy, having adequate insurance is of critical importance. This coverage could range from health to life and disability, home, auto or umbrella, to protect against property loss or damage.

3. Diversify your investments

Diversification is an approach to risk management that involves spreading your investments across sectors and categories evenly while optimizing your returns by selecting areas that would respond differently to the same events or accidents. The aim is to maximize returns through this hedging technique by diversifying into various instruments that will respond differently to the same unforeseen event.

4. Make a succession plan

This means making certain that all the legal documents needed for succession are up to date and in place. They could be wills, powers of attorney or healthcare directives. These legal instruments will ensure that your wishes will be carried out in the matter of your wealth upon your death or incapacitation.

Financial contingency plans shouldn't remain static. Instead, they should be reviewed regularly and adjusted based on the changes in your financial situation, your family structure and your life goals. At its heart, contingency planning is all about planning for what could come your way; it is about taking measures so that if a crisis does happen you won't struggle alone to cope financially. Although you cannot predict every crisis that can possibly come your way, you can always be prepared to deal with any crisis that might come up.

Building an Emergency Fund

An emergency fund should form the cornerstone of any sound financial plan, acting as an insurance policy against sudden emergencies such as job loss, illness or repairs that may arise unexpectedly. In India, three to twelve months' living expenses are generally recommended as an ideal emergency savings target, but this could differ, depending on individual circumstances.

Calculating the size of your emergency fund

The key thing to fix about an emergency fund is its size. First, determine your monthly expenses such as rent or EMI payments, utility bills, groceries, commute, children's educational fees and miscellaneous expenditures. Multiply these numbers by three to nine if your job lacks stability; for sole earners, this number may be as high as twelve!

Building your fund

Now that you have determined how much you need to save for your emergency fund, the next step is to accumulate it. Set aside a portion from your monthly income—anywhere between 5 per cent and 10 per cent, or even up to 50 per cent. It should be as high as you can make it. Prioritize savings as mandatory expenses.

Where should my emergency fund be kept?

An emergency fund should be easily accessible and safe from market instability. Here are a few options for Indians living in India.

1. Savings account

A regular savings account offers easy access to funds and also earns you a nominal interest. Some banks provide higher yields than others on savings accounts. But remember, the purpose of an emergency fund is to act as an emergency safety net rather than to create wealth through interest earned on it.

2. Cash

For your immediate needs, keeping part of your emergency fund in the form of physical cash could prove beneficial, though keeping too much could pose the risk of theft or damage. Additionally, cash doesn't have any interest-earning potential.

3. Fixed deposits (FDs)

In India, fixed deposits have long been considered safe investments that offer higher interest rates than savings accounts and can even be broken before their tenure ends for emergency needs. Any early-withdrawal penalties tend to be offset by the accrued earnings, and penalties on early withdrawal of funds from an FD are in general lower than for other types of accounts.

4. Liquid mutual funds

Liquid mutual funds are an excellent way of building up emergency savings funds. Typically investing in short-term market instruments like treasury bills and government securities with minimal risks, these mutual funds don't encumber you with lock-in periods and typically offer greater returns than savings accounts or fixed deposits (FDs). The redemption process, though, may take some time (an estimated twenty-four to forty-eight hours, generally).

5. Sweep-in fixed deposits

Certain banks in India provide this facility whereby any excess balance in your savings accounts is automatically converted into an FD for increased returns, with funds then liquidating back into savings when needed and providing liquidity as well as higher yields for better liquidity management and returns. This instrument provides liquidity combined with improved returns.

6. Recurring deposits (RDs)

Do you find it challenging to set aside large sums quickly? Recurring deposits may be the solution for you. Simply deposit an equal sum every month into an RD; interest accrues, as in fixed deposit accounts, and helps you build your savings over time.

Remember, an emergency fund's main objective is not wealth accumulation but to serve as a safety net against unexpected expenses. Once you've created one, any extra savings can be routed through appropriate investment channels to help you meet your financial goals. Creating an emergency fund perhaps calls for patience and dedication but will bring you peace of mind during tough financial times. Start today by setting aside a sum of money from your earnings, even if it is small. Over time, your emergency funds will grow and help protect you during times of unpredictable expenses!

Case study: Ravi Singh—Establishing an Emergency Fund

Background

Ravi Singh, a thirty-five-year-old software engineer residing in Bengaluru, is the sole breadwinner of his family, consisting of his wife and two young children, Ravi earns a good income but hasn't considered the importance of an emergency fund until recently, when he had a conversation with someone who had lost his job when his company downsized.

Calculating the size of the emergency fund

Ravi has estimated his family's monthly expenses at around Rs 50,000. This includes the rent, groceries, utilities, school fees for his two sons, transportation and miscellaneous expenses. As he is the sole earner in the family, he decides that his emergency fund must cover twelve months' expenses and would thus have to be at least Rs 6 lakh.

Building the fund

Ravi has conducted an exhaustive budget review and is determined to set aside Rs 30,000 each month towards his emergency fund without altering the family's current lifestyle in any significant way. At this saving rate, it will take him twenty months to reach his target amount of Rs 6 lakh.

Storing the emergency fund

Ravi chooses an approach with multiple components for his emergency fund:

1. Savings account

He keeps Rs 60,000 in an immediate-access savings account as part of his emergency fund.

2. Cash

Ravi keeps Rs 30,000 in cash at home to cover immediate unforeseen expenses that may require payment in cash.

3. Fixed deposit

He opens a fixed deposit with his bank for Rs 2,10,000. The deposit offers him better interest earnings than traditional savings accounts, yet can be broken at any time in an emergency.

4. Liquid mutual fund

Ravi has invested Rs 3 lakh in a liquid mutual fund as it offers higher returns than an FD or a savings account and redemption too is relatively straightforward.

Outcome of Ravi's efforts to create an emergency fund

Let's now consider two scenarios after the emergency fund has been established:

Scenario 1: No emergency situation arises

It has been three years since Ravi built his emergency fund. Thankfully, there were no emergency situations in the last three years and the emergency fund has now grown to Rs 6,60,000. Ravi can withdraw the excess Rs 60,000 from this fund and invest towards other financial goals.

Scenario 2: Ravi loses his job

Given the market conditions, Ravi loses his IT job and it takes six months to find another one. The emergency fund will help pay for his living expenses during these difficult six months without a job but its value will reduce from Rs 6 lakh to Rs 3 lakh. Ravi will start investing again in the emergency fund from the salary income of the new job. Assuming he can now save Rs 60,000 every month towards the emergency fund, it will take him another five months to restore the emergency fund to its target value.

The lesson

Ravi's story highlights the value of creating and maintaining an emergency fund as part of one's personal financial strategy. It is important to save, but it is also important to consider where the money saved can be stored so that it can make all the difference during emergency situations while earning some returns.

Insurance

Insurance plays a pivotal role in financial planning by protecting you against unexpected events. Health and life policies are among the most essential types of coverage offered in India.

Health insurance in India

Health insurance provides crucial protection of your finances when you must incur medical expenses related to illnesses or injuries that result in costly treatments, and healthcare costs are only growing higher each day in India, making comprehensive health coverage even more essential for individuals and their families.

There are various health insurance plans available in India:

1. Individual health insurance

This covers health costs up to the sum insured for one individual policyholder.

2. Family floater health insurance

This policy covers an entire family under one plan and distributes its coverage across its members evenly. All family members covered under it contribute equally towards the payout.

3. Super top-up health insurance

A super top-up health insurance policy is a type of health insurance that provides additional coverage beyond the sum insured of an existing health insurance policy. It acts as a supplementary cover, coming into play when the medical expenses exceed the threshold limit of the primary health insurance policy. Super top-up policies are useful for individuals who want to enhance their health coverage without buying an entirely new primary health insurance policy with a higher sum insured. They help in increasing the coverage limit without significantly increasing the insurance premium amount.

4. Health insurance for senior citizens

Senior Citizen Health Insurance covers medical expenses incurred by people above sixty years of age. It covers pre-existing diseases and offers preventive health check-up facilities to the elderly and cashless hospitalization at network hospitals of the insurance company.

Pradhan Mantri Jan Arogya Yojana (PM-JAY) is the most comprehensive government-funded health insurance scheme for senior citizens as well as women and children in India. As a component of the Ayushman Bharat campaign, it aims at providing insurance and securing healthcare for all the members of the family.

5. Critical illness insurance

This insurance offers a lump-sum payout should one be diagnosed with one of the specific critical illnesses specified in the policy.

6. Maternity coverage

When considering your maternity protection needs it's essential that both the mother and father get covered under one policy if possible. This policy covers costs associated with childbirth and pre/postnatal care.

Consider factors like coverage limit, inclusions/exclusions, network of hospitals, waiting period for pre-existing diseases, premium amount and claim settlement ratio when purchasing a health insurance policy. Furthermore, most policies come with an annual deductible, which must be paid before your coverage kicks in.

Additionally, under Section 80D of the Indian Income-tax Act, premiums paid towards health insurance qualify for tax deduction, making health coverage and planning an invaluable exercise as part of financial planning.

Case study: Uday Mishra: Super Top-Up Health Insurance

Background

Uday Mishra, a forty-five-year-old resident of Mumbai, recognizes the need for increased health insurance because of the rising healthcare costs and their unpredictable nature. Although already possessing basic coverage through an existing plan, he wishes to get additional financial protection for himself and his family by adding a super top-up policy coverage to it.

Policy details:

- Basic health insurance: Sum insured—Rs 5 lakh with deductible of Rs 50,000
- Super top-up insurance: Sum insured—Rs 10 lakh with deductible of Rs 5 lakh
- Policy Term: 1 year

Scenario 1: Minor hospitalization expenses

Unfortunately, Uday undergoes a minor surgery that leads to medical expenses of Rs 4 lakh. The amount is within the basic insurance limit, so the basic insurance provider pays Rs 3.5 lakh to the hospital while Uday has to pay Rs 50,000. The super top-up insurance is not applicable in this case since the medical expense of Rs 4 lakh is below the deductible amount of Rs 5 lakh.

Scenario 2: Major hospitalization expenses

Uday's wife requires hospitalization for a major medical procedure leading to medical expenses of Rs 9 lakh. The basic insurance provider will pay Rs 4.5 lakh to the hospital while Uday will have to pay Rs 50,000. The amount in excess of the deductible of Rs 4 lakh (i.e., Rs 9 lakh minus Rs 5 lakh) will be paid by super top-up insurance. Thus, both insurances combined pay Rs 8.5 lakh while Uday only pays Rs 50,000.

By opting for a super top-up health insurance policy, Uday has been able to enhance his existing coverage at a relatively reduced premium compared with purchasing an independent comprehensive plan. It has provided him with additional financial protection against major medical expenses, bringing his entire family peace of mind and protection.

Note that this case study is fictional and is only an illustration. The actual benefits, terms and conditions of super top-up health insurance policies will depend on which provider and policy one selects. Before making your final decision on purchasing any policy, you should carefully assess all the details regarding coverage options as well as exclusions to make sure it fits with your individual financial goals and meets your requirements.

Life insurance in India

Life insurance policies provide policyholders and insurers alike with peace of mind upon the death of the insured individual. In return for this promise made by the insurer, premium payments from the policyholder are made, either regularly or as an upfront sum. There are various types of life policies available across India. We list some of them here:

1. Term life insurance

This form of life insurance provides for easy payout if the policyholder passes away during its term; otherwise, there will be no payout to the nominee or estate.

2. Endowment policies

This type of life insurance policy serves a dual purpose by providing both life insurance cover and a savings or investment component. It is a combination of insurance protection and a savings plan. The policy pays a lump sum amount to the beneficiary in the event of the policyholder's death during the term of the policy. If the policyholder survives the entire policy term (maturity), they receive the maturity benefit, which is the sum assured plus the accumulated bonus or returns from the investment portion.

3. Unit-linked insurance plans (ULIPs)

These investments combine insurance and investment. A portion of the premium is allocated towards life cover while the rest may be invested in equity, debt, or a mix thereof.

4. Whole life insurance

This kind of policy offers protection throughout a person's lifetime and has both a death benefit payout and a savings component that grows steadily over time.

What insurance policy you select will depend on your financial goals, your risk tolerance and your dependants' financial needs. Term insurance provides high coverage at low premiums and is ideal if you have financial dependants, while investment-oriented policies such as endowment plans or ULIPs could offer tax breaks up to a specified limit under Section 80C of India's Income-tax Act.

Overall, health and life insurance are indispensable components of financial planning in India. While health insurance helps cover high medical costs, life insurance provides security to your dependants should something happen to you. Before making a decision on what insurance policy to take, it's essential to evaluate your needs carefully while understanding all the features offered by the various available policies. A financial adviser or insurance specialist could assist you in selecting suitable policies tailored specifically to your circumstances.

Case study: Sunita Agarwal—Insurance Planning Process

Background

Sunita Agarwal is a forty-year-old HR professional living in Mumbai. She is married and the primary earner in the family. Sunita had not bought any health or life insurance policy until she witnessed the financial struggles of a close friend after an unexpected health crisis. That was a wake-up call, prompting Sunita to purchase protection for both herself and her loved ones.

Sunita conducted research before opting for a family floater health insurance plan, believing that a single policy covering her entire family would be both cost-effective and easier to administer. Her policy, with an insured sum of Rs 10 lakh, covered hospitalization expenses as well as pre/post hospitalization costs and day-care procedures while offering cashless treatment at over 3600 hospitals nationwide.

She wanted coverage for critical illnesses but quickly discovered her chosen health insurance plan did not offer enough. Therefore, she purchased an additional critical-illness policy with an annual sum insured of Rs 20 lakh, which covered cancer, heart disease, stroke and kidney failure, among other diseases, offering financial protection should critical health events arise. Upon diagnosis of one or more of the illnesses covered under her critical illness policy, she will receive an immediate lump-sum payment as financial security against major events that might impact her family's well-being.

Acquiring a life insurance policy

Sunita chose a term life policy with an annual cover of Rs 1 crore to protect her family financially in case she were to pass suddenly. Her plan was cost-effective and provided the family peace of mind, as they knew they would have financial security even in her absence. Sunita also added accidental death riders for additional coverage.

Outcome

Years later, Sunita was diagnosed with an urgent heart condition which required immediate surgery. Thanks to health insurance coverage of most of the medical expenses incurred and coverage of her recovery and the critical illness policy benefits that paid her a lump sum, there wasn't any strain on the family's finances as she recovered.

Tragically, Sunita died two years after her recovery in a car accident. While her family grieved their emotional loss, the term insurance payout of Rs 1 crore provided them substantial financial support while the accidental death rider provided them extra funds so they could maintain their lifestyle without financial strain, and Sunita's children could continue their studies unhindered.

Lessons

Sunita's case study illustrates the value of both health and life insurance in an individual's financial plan. Her combination of family floater health insurance with critical illness cover ensured that her sudden health crisis didn't derail their finances; and her wise investments in term insurance policies ensured that her family would still have financial protection even after her passing, providing them security during uncertain times. Her case highlights the essential role of insurance in managing risks and protecting individuals and families during times of uncertainty.

Diversification

Diversification is an investment strategy to manage risk by spreading investments across various financial instruments, sectors and other categories. Diversification aims to offset unpredictable events within a portfolio by spreading the positive returns among different investments against any negative returns that might occur in the portfolio, thus mitigating negative events with equal but positive results across investments in the portfolio.

Diversification can encompass numerous investment avenues and investors have many choices. Some of the common investment avenues are equity, mutual funds, bonds and debentures, Public Provident Fund (PPF), National Pension System (NPS), Kisan Vikas Patra (KVP), National Savings Certificate (NSC), fixed deposits (FD) and recurring deposits (RD), real estate and gold.

Indian investors are also diversifying geographically. An increase in the permissible level of investment in foreign equities and mutual funds allows Indian investors to capitalize on global opportunities while protecting themselves against currency risk.

Strategizing on the diversification options available today

Successful investment diversification means the selection of assets that perform differently under various market conditions. This keeps your portfolio balanced so that if one investment underperforms, its shortcomings are offset by positive returns from other investments.

The diversification must match an investor's financial goals, risk tolerance and time horizon. A young investor with an aggressive risk tolerance looking to amass wealth may opt for heavily diversified equities and mutual funds in his or her portfolio. An older individual seeking stable income might diversify with bonds, fixed deposits and real estate instead.

Diversification of investments can help reduce risk and volatility, but it should not be used as a fail-safe method against losses in declining markets. Furthermore, over-diversification could result in average returns and can make your portfolio challenging to manage.

Diversification is the cornerstone of financial planning in India. While diversification can seem daunting at first, its key importance cannot be overstated. It requires periodic review and adjustments based on market conditions as well as personal circumstances, so working with an adviser to create and manage an optimally diversified portfolio that aligns with one's financial goals and risk tolerance is key for long-term investment success.

Case study: Arjun Gupta—Diversifying Investments in India

Background

Arjun Gupta, thirty, is an Indian software developer living in Pune. He has been saving a significant portion of his earnings without an explicit plan, but has decided it is time to use his savings strategically and make investments that will grow his wealth.

Initial investment approach

Arjun initially invests exclusively in fixed deposits and Public Provident Fund (PPF), as they carry lower risk than other options. When it becomes clear that these investments alone may not produce the returns necessary to meet his long-term financial goals, Arjun decides to diversify his portfolio further.

Arjun's diversified portfolio

Arjun meets with his financial adviser and gets a diversified investment plan based on his risk profile and financial goals. His investments are divided as follows:

1. Equity

Thirty per cent of his investments are used to purchase shares across different sectors like IT, pharmaceuticals and manufacturing. He chooses a mix of large-, mid- and small-capitalization companies in order to balance risk against returns.

2. Mutual funds

Thirty per cent of his funds are allocated for mutual fund purchases. Arjun buys several equity mutual funds (large-cap and mid-cap equity funds, balanced funds and debt funds, considering his risk appetite and financial goals).

3. Fixed deposits and PPF

Arjun sets aside 20 per cent of his funds in fixed deposits and PPF accounts to guarantee safe and steady returns over time.

4. Real estate

He invests 10 per cent of his funds to purchase an apartment in an up-and-coming suburb that promises excellent long-term returns.

5. Gold

Gold ETFs are selected as his gold asset allocation solution of choice because of their liquid market presence and safety features. Arjun allocated 5 per cent of his funds to gold.

6. International diversification

Arjun divides 5 per cent of his investments among US technology company shares as an international diversification element.

Outcome

Ten years later, as IT growth explodes, Arjun's equity investments and mutual funds focused on this industry provide him with significant returns. Significant real estate appreciation has occurred due to infrastructural improvements close to where he has purchased residential property. Unfortunately, some of his mid-cap and small-cap equities have underperformed and his debt mutual funds have brought lower returns than usual during one period, as a result of lower interest rates than anticipated. But, overall, success is realized from these investments, though ten years later than expected!

Arjun's portfolio has been marked by ups and downs over time; yet his returns have grown steadily overall, showing the effectiveness of diversification in generating returns over time. His fixed deposits and PPF provide him with steady returns while his investments in US equities have flourished because of the global technology boom.

Lessons

Arjun's journey as an investor underlines the significance of diversification as part of any effective investment plan. By diversifying his investments across asset classes, sectors and even geographies, Arjun has been able to successfully navigate market volatility while watching his wealth expand over time. Diversification may not totally prevent losses, but can certainly help manage risks while potentially increasing returns—something that Arjun has proved through his journey of becoming an exceptional example of long-term financial success in India.

Succession Planning

Succession planning, or estate planning, refers to the practice of creating an orderly transition of wealth and assets from one generation or beneficiary to the next. Succession planning in India is especially critical due to the complex laws surrounding inheritance and property rights.

Tools for succession planning

1. The will

A will is a legally enforceable document which details how assets should be distributed after the will-maker's death and is often the cornerstone of succession planning in India. For it to be legally effective, however, it must be written clearly, signed by its creator (known as the testator) and witnessed by at least two individuals. Its registration under Indian law, however, is optional.

2. The trust

A trust is a legal arrangement where one party (the settlor) transfers assets to another (the trustee) for use by third-party beneficiaries who benefit. Trusts provide an efficient means of managing and passing down wealth and are particularly beneficial when it comes to managing the accounts of minors, of those with special needs, or those handling large estates.

3. Gifts

Lifetime gifting is another means of transferring property. A person may transfer assets or property as gifts directly to the beneficiaries who will benefit from it. According to India's Gift Act, gifts made directly between relatives (as defined under the Income-tax Act) are exempted from tax.

4. Joint ownership

Assets can be held jointly with the right of survivorship so that if one owner dies, his or her share in the asset automatically transfers to those remaining who hold joint ownership with survivorship rights.

5. Life insurance

Proceeds from life insurance can provide financial security to dependants after someone dies and can also be used to settle outstanding debts, protecting an estate for future beneficiaries.

6. The Hindu Undivided Family (HUF)

Under Hindu law, an HUF is defined as an unincorporated legal entity comprising its eldest member and his or her descendants. The property of such an HUF is administered by its *karta*; upon his/her passing away, the successor becomes the karta and so on.

Challenges in succession planning

People often encounter difficulties in succession planning in India because of low awareness, complex family structures and unwillingness to discuss death and inheritance matters openly. Mismanagement of assets, family disputes and court battles often arise as a result of insufficient succession planning.

The famous legal dispute over the succession of the M.P. Birla Group is an excellent case in point.*

Importance of professional guidance

As succession laws and tax implications become more complicated, professional guidance for succession planning becomes essential. Lawyers, chartered accountants and financial planners can assist individuals in creating an effective succession plan that ensures smooth transfer of their assets and minimizes tax liabilities while also preventing legal disputes.

Conclusion

Succession planning is an integral component of financial and wealth management in India, serving to ensure that a person's hard-earned wealth is distributed according to his or her wishes and provides security to loved ones. Due to evolving family dynamics and increased wealth creation, effective succession planning has never been more essential. Regardless of the estate size or value they own, everyone should create a succession plan so their wealth is transferred without incident to the intended beneficiaries and without disputes arising over legal complexities or property laws. The earlier such planning starts taking effect, the easier it will be to deal with complex succession laws or

---

* The tussle between the Birlas and Lodhas started in 2004 after the then-chairman of Birla Corporation, Priyamvada Birla, died. Following her death, Rajendra Singh Lodha, co-chairman and chartered accountant of the company, produced her will, as of 1999, which read that her Rs 5000-crore assets be bequeathed to him. It also assigned R.S. Lodha as the head of M.P. Birla Group companies. This version of the will was strongly contested by the Birlas, who in turn, claimed that in July 1983, Priyamvada Birla and M.P. Birla had created a mutual will. As per this will, the estate fortune would be distributed for charity among the Hindustan Medical Institution, Eastern India Educational Institution and the M.P. Birla Foundation. The legal battle continues now for eighteen years!

potential litigation claims and lawsuits over who owns how much of what asset or property.

Case study: Ramesh Verma—Succession Planning

Background

Ramesh Verma, a resident of Delhi, has amassed a substantial estate during his lifetime. This includes an established textile business and numerous properties across Delhi and Mumbai and substantial investments in fixed deposits, stocks and mutual funds. His family includes his wife, two sons, one daughter and two grandsons. Realizing the complexity of his estate and the potential for family disputes, he seeks professional guidance for succession planning.

1. Making a will

Ramesh prepares his will with assistance from his lawyer. In its detailed contents, he lays down how his properties and business should be distributed among his two sons equally in terms of shares in the textile business. The Mumbai property will go to his daughter while the primary residence will remain with his wife as her inheritance.

2. Creating a trust

In order to provide financial security for his grandsons, he sets up a trust. The dividends from his substantial mutual fund investments are transferred directly into this account, and its trustee, his eldest son, is charged with using these funds for the children's education and welfare.

3. Gifts

To circumvent potential tax liabilities, Ramesh has gifted some of his shares in various businesses to his children already.

These transfers are exempted from tax, as per Indian Gift Act regulations.

4. Creating joint ownership of assets

Ramesh owns numerous fixed deposits and bonds held jointly with his wife under an 'Either or Survivor' clause, so these investments will pass to her upon his death without legal hassles or complications.

5. Taking a life insurance policy

Ramesh has taken out a substantial life insurance policy and has nominated his wife as the beneficiary. This ensures that she will have financial support following his passing.

Outcome

Ten years after making these arrangements, Ramesh passes away peacefully, knowing he has done all he can to ensure the smooth succession of his estate. Thanks to his comprehensive and legally sound succession plan, his assets are distributed according to his wishes without any family disputes, leaving his wife living comfortably off their once jointly owned assets and his life insurance proceeds. The textile business is run efficiently under his sons' leadership and the daughter has received her rightful share of the family property without issue or dispute.

His grandsons who are still minors have their financial future secured, thanks to the trust. Not only has the generous gift they have received brought happiness into their lives but it has also reduced the inheritance tax bill for them significantly.

Lessons

Ramesh Verma's estate planning is an outstanding illustration of the effectiveness of succession planning in India's context, with wills, trusts, gifting and life insurance products featuring as elements in his comprehensive succession plan. His story highlights the importance of early and effective succession planning to prevent family disputes while guaranteeing fair distribution of assets as well as providing financial security to loved ones. It also underscores the importance of seeking professional guidance in confronting complex estate and succession laws.

Key takeaways from this section

1. Draw up your financial goals using the SMART framework
2. Categorize your goals based on their time horizons
3. Prioritize your goals
4. Determine the cost of your goals, accounting for inflation
5. Determine what your investment instruments will be, based on your time horizons and risk profile
6. Determine the amount of savings needed for each goal
7. Allocate your savings to your goals based on their priority
   - Drop or defer low-priority goals
8. Plan for contingencies
   - Have your emergency fund and insurance policies in place
9. Plan for succession

Section 3: Take Action (T)

'The future depends on what you do today.'
—Mahatma Gandhi

Taking action once a financial plan is in place is, of course, crucial for its success. This involves implementing the budget, saving regularly, investing as per the plan, reviewing your progress periodically and making the necessary adjustments to the plan. Action ensures that the plan becomes a reality, leading to financial stability and the achievement of long-term goals.

Chapter 7

Create a Budget

Projecting income

Income projection is essential when creating a financial plan and budget and will provide you an accurate picture of how much you have available for expenses, savings and investments. Here's an outline of how to forecast income for creating a budget:

1. Understand your income sources

As part of this initial step, identify all your sources of income, both active (regular salary from employment) and passive (side gig, rental income, dividends from investments, pensions, alimony, royalties, etc.), when projecting your future income.

2. Estimate your consistent income

If you are employed full-time in a steady, salaried job, estimation of your income should be straightforward. Focus on after-tax or net income to get an accurate picture. This money represents how much is actually coming home each month and can be considered for budgeting purposes.

3. Account for variable income

This is a more challenging exercise, but still possible. Review your income over the last six to twelve months to get an idea of your regular earnings. You could compute an average monthly figure or use your lowest-earning month as a conservative baseline to make your projections.

4. Annual bonuses or commissions

When creating income projections for yourself and/or your family, be sure to factor in annual bonuses, commissions and similar income. Since these can fluctuate wildly and often don't come through reliably, consider them when you do get them as extra savings rather than counting on them as part of regular budgeting, or include a conservative estimate in your projections instead.

5. Projected income increases

If you anticipate a raise, promotion or increased business profits soon enough, it might tempt you to include them in your income projections and budget accordingly. But until confirmation of these raises takes place, it's usually best to budget on the basis of only your current income and make adjustments later when the changes actually come about.

6. Inflation

When making long-term financial plans, it's crucial to take inflation into account, particularly if your income sources include investments or rental properties. Over time, money loses value; therefore, the same amount today will buy less tomorrow than it will today. Whenever possible, include reasonable estimates of inflation when projecting income streams.

7. Tax considerations

Taxes can have an enormous effect on your net income. Be sure you have in-depth knowledge of all your obligations related to income tax, self-employment tax, if applicable (freelancer/

entrepreneurs only) and any other local taxes before creating income projections.

8. Utilize financial tools

There are various financial tools and software solutions that can assist you with income projection, helping ensure accuracy while saving you both time and effort.

Case study: Virat Mamnani—Projecting Income

Background

Virat Mamnani, thirty-two, living in Noida, is a software developer. He earns an annual salary of Rs 12 lakh at the multinational company he works for and is seeking a comprehensive financial plan to prepare for his marriage next year. His first step towards financial planning is a projection of his future income while taking into consideration factors like annual salary increases, changes in his personal life circumstances, inflation rates and taxation considerations.

1. Current income

Virat's primary source of income is his annual salary of Rs 12 lakh. He has other sources of income, such as interest from his savings account and fixed deposits that yield an annual amount of Rs 30,000. His total current annual income stands at about Rs 12.3 lakh.

2. Anticipated increment

Based on the past pattern at his workplace, Virat anticipates an average annual increment of about 10 per cent in his salary. This amount accounts for his regular salary increase.

3. Personal life changes

Virat plans to marry his long-term companion next year. She is working as a teacher in an international school. He conservatively estimates her annual income at around Rs 8 lakh, which will add to their combined income.

4. Inflation

Over time, inflation erodes the purchasing power of money and will directly and negatively affect Virat's income while indirectly impacting expenses and savings values. To ensure that his lifestyle remains sustainable, Virat needs his income to increase at a pace greater than inflation, which typically runs at 5–7 per cent per annum in India.

5. Taxation

As Virat falls in the 30 per cent tax bracket, his earnings increase will also likely be subjected to tax at 30 per cent. However, there may be options available under Sections 80C (for long-term investments), 80D (for medical insurance), 10(14) (for HRA allowance) and more of the Income-tax Act that can help decrease his taxable income and potentially lower his overall burden of taxes.

Given these considerations, here's how Virat projects his income for the next two years:

Year 1

- *Salary post-increment:* Rs 12 lakh + 10% of Rs 12 lakh = Rs 13.2 lakh
- *Other income (interest):* Rs 30,000
- *Spouse's income:* Rs 8 lakh
- *Total household income:* Rs 13.2 lakh + Rs 30,000 + Rs 8 lakh = Rs 21.5 lakh

Year 2

- *Salary post-increment:* Rs 13.2 lakh + 10% of Rs 13.2 lakh = Rs 14.52 lakh

- *Spouse's salary post 12% increment:* Rs 8.8 lakh
- *Total household income:* Rs 14.52 lakh + Rs 30,000 + Rs 8.8 lakh = Rs 23.32 lakh

Virat uses tax planning strategies and exemptions to minimize his taxable income and work towards fulfilling his financial goals. He consults a tax adviser for effective planning to achieve these goals, projecting his income over time and taking all the above-mentioned factors into consideration so he gets a holistic picture of his future financial standing. This way he can plan his savings, investments and expenditures appropriately. He considers inflation too in his plans so that his wealth will grow in real terms.

Conclusion

In summary, Virat's approach towards income projection is comprehensive and realistic, taking all key financial elements into consideration to create an achievable financial plan for himself and his family's future security.

Projecting expenses

Estimating future expenses is essential to creating a comprehensive financial plan and budget. Accurate projections will allow you to prepare for both expected and unexpected expenses. Here's an easy way you can project your future expenses using your current spending patterns:

1. Determine current expenses

Start by creating a comprehensive list of your current expenses. Include fixed costs such as rent/loan payments, insurance premiums and utilities as well as variable expenses like groceries, transportation and entertainment/discretionary spending in this category. You should use bank statements, credit card bills and receipts so that all your expenditure is taken into account.

2. Categorize your expenses

Categorizing your expenses on housing, utilities, groceries, health, entertainment and other items will enable you to keep an accurate account of where your money is going and identify areas in which there may be overspending.

3. Calculate your average monthly expenses

Calculate an average monthly cost in each category to deal with the variable expenses, such as on utilities or groceries. It is wise to use at least six months' data in this exercise to make accurate estimates.

4. Include seasonal expenses in your projections

Account for seasonal expenses like electricity costs,[*] holidays, festival gifts and travel in your projections.

5. Account for infrequent expenses

Certain expenses such as car maintenance or property taxes don't occur monthly but still need to be factored into your budget. Divide their yearly costs by twelve and incorporate this figure into your budget plan.

6. Plan for inflation

Over time, inflation can alter the cost of goods and services, so as part of any long-term financial plan, it is wise to factor in what the impact may be in terms of expenses in future years. The typical rate of inflation is 5 to 7 per cent per annum.

---

[*] For example, high electricity consumption due to the usage of air conditioning during summer.

7. Keep life changes in mind

Be sure to consider any upcoming life changes that might impact your expenses. This could be moving into a new home or city, starting a family, purchasing property or retiring. They can significantly change how and what you spend money on.

8. Future goals

If your financial plans include saving for a vacation, car purchase or retirement savings, these should also be added to the expenses category.

9. Emergency fund

Saving up to create an emergency fund that covers three to twelve months' living expenses should always be your goal when budgeting for emergencies or unexpected costs.

10. Debt repayment

When planning expenses, be sure to include repayments of home loan, student loan or credit card debt as part of your expenses. To accelerate their repayment, set aside additional budget items specifically for debt-reduction expenses.

11. Review and adjust your plan

Your expenses can change over time, so a regular budget review and adjustment process is vital to keeping it accurate and relevant.

12. Utilize financial tools

There are various budgeting apps and financial planning tools that can assist you in projecting your future expenses accurately. They allow users to track their spending patterns, organize expenses into categories and produce accurate projections for any unforeseen costs that might come their way.

Accurate projection of future expenses will allow you to develop an accurate financial plan so you can live within your means, save for the future and meet your financial goals. Although it might require time and effort, understanding where your money goes is the key to taking control of your future. Your expenses should be kept under review and revision should occur regularly as your circumstances evolve. Keep your budget alive; review it often as your situation shifts!

Case study: Rohan Singh—Projecting Expenses

Background

Rohan Singh is an Indian software engineer living in Bengaluru and earning a monthly payout of Rs 1 lakh after tax deductions.

Step 1: Identification of current expenses

After reviewing his expenses for the past six months, Rohan has found that his average monthly expenses are as follows:

- Rent: Rs 25,000
- Utilities (including electricity, the Internet and cell phone): Rs 5000
- Groceries: Rs 8000
- Transportation (fuel, car maintenance): Rs 6000
- Health insurance premium: Rs 2000
- Eating out and entertainment: Rs 7000
- Miscellaneous expenses: Rs 5000

Step 2: Categorization of expenses

Rohan then categorizes his expenses into fixed and variable ones. Rent, utilities and health insurance are his fixed expenses. Groceries, transportation, eating out, entertainment and miscellaneous expenses fall under variable expenses.

Step 3: Calculation of average monthly costs

Rohan has done this already in Step 1. His total monthly expenditure is Rs 58,000.

Step 4: Seasonal expenses

Rohan spends more on utilities during summer because of the increased use of air conditioning. He also spends more on travel during the holiday seasons. He adjusts his utility and travel expenses accordingly.

Step 5: Infrequent expenses

Rohan's car insurance premium is Rs 12,000 per year, and he usually spends around Rs 10,000 per year on car maintenance. This adds another Rs 1833 (Rs 22,000 divided by 12) to his monthly expenses.

Step 6: Inflation

Rohan considers an average inflation rate of 5 per cent per year for calculating his future expenses, which is around the average inflation rate in India.

Step 7: Life changes

Rohan plans to get married in the next two years. This is likely to increase his monthly expenses as he will be supporting a family. He estimates his monthly expenses may increase by around 30 per cent.

Step 8: Future goals

Rohan's goal is to buy an apartment in five years. He estimates he'll need Rs 30 lakh for the down payment. He starts saving Rs 50,000 per month towards this goal.

Step 9: Emergency fund

Rohan aims to build an emergency fund that can cover six months' living expenses, which totals Rs 3,48,000 (Rs 58,000 times 6). He decides to set aside Rs 14,500 each month for this purpose.

Step 10: Debt repayment

Rohan has no current debts, but he knows that if he takes a home loan in the future, he will have to add the repayment instalments to his monthly expenses.

Step 11: Review and adjustment

Rohan will review his expense projection every three months to check if he's on track and make the necessary adjustments.

Step 12: Use of financial tools

Rohan uses a financial planning app to track his spending and savings, and this helps him stay on top of his budget.

So, in summary, Rohan's total monthly expenses, including savings for future goals and emergencies, come to Rs 1,24,333. This is more than his current income, so he knows he needs to either cut back on some expenses, increase his income or adjust his savings goals. This kind of detailed projection helps Rohan make informed decisions about his financial future.

Process of finalizing goals and computing savings to achieve them

Finalizing goals and computing the savings required to achieve them is a key part of financial planning. Let's consider Kavita Pawar, a thirty-year-old marketing manager living in Mumbai, to illustrate this process.

Step 1: Identification of financial goals

Kavita begins by identifying her short-term, medium-term and long-term financial goals.

- *Short-term goal (1–3 years):* She plans to buy a car costing Rs 8 lakh in two years
- *Medium-term goal (3–7 years):* She plans to pursue an MBA from a top-tier institution, which she estimates will cost about Rs 20 lakh in today's value in five years
- *Long-term goal (7+ years):* She wants to save Rs 2 crore for her retirement at age sixty

Step 2: Inflation adjustment

Next, Kavita adjusts these goals for inflation since the cost of her goals will rise over time. Assuming an average inflation rate of 5 per cent, her goals become:

- *Car:* Rs 8 lakh * $(1.05)^2$ = Rs 8.82 lakh
- *MBA:* Rs 20 lakh * $(1.05)^5$ = Rs 25.52 lakh
- *Retirement:* Assuming her retirement is thirty years away and the retirement corpus would need to sustain her for another twenty-five years, computing this gets a bit complex. It's advisable for Kavita to use the retirement calculators available online, but Kavita's objective is to ensure that her corpus can provide her with a substantial inflation-adjusted income throughout her retirement.

Step 3: Calculating monthly savings

Kavita then determines how much she needs to save each month to meet these goals, using either an Excel function or a financial calculator. She estimates an annual return rate of 8 per cent from her investments. She figures the following:

- *Car:* To accumulate Rs 8.82 lakh in two years, she needs to save approximately Rs 35,500 per month
- *MBA:* To accumulate Rs 25.52 lakh in five years, she needs to save around Rs 36,250 per month
- *Retirement:* The exact monthly savings will depend on various factors, including her expected lifespan, retirement lifestyle, etc. For this purpose, it's best to use an online retirement calculator

Step 4: Review and adjustments

Kavita reviews her financial goals and savings plan annually to stay abreast of changes to her income, expenses and life circumstances that necessitate the adaption of her plans accordingly.

Step 5: Utilization of financial tools

Kavita utilizes an app-based financial planning solution to track her savings and her progress towards her goals, in addition to consulting a personal financial adviser for personalized guidance and advice.

Step 6: Actual saving and investing

Kavita then begins saving and investing, going by the guidelines put in place, setting up automatic transfers into her savings and investment accounts to stay true to her plan.

In summary, Kavita can reach her financial goals by setting goals, accounting for inflation, computing her required monthly savings amounts and then regularly reviewing and revising her plan. Kavita understands this is a dynamic process which may need adjustments to be made from time to time, but will adapt her plans as necessary so she stays on the path towards meeting them.

Chapter 8

Create an Investment Plan

Asset allocation

Asset allocation is an integral component of financial planning. This process entails diversification of investments across different kinds of assets to maximize returns while mitigating risk, typically dividing them among various asset classes such as stocks, bonds, real estate or commodities, depending on your risk tolerance, your timeline for investing and your overall goals.

Here are a few major asset classes in India:

1. Equities/stocks

Equity investments provide ownership in companies and may offer higher long-term returns than other asset classes, although their values can fluctuate rapidly. They can further be classified by company size as large-, mid- and small-cap equities.

2. Debt/bonds

These investments tend to be safer investments that involve lending money directly to a government or corporation for an agreed-upon term at a predetermined interest rate. They provide steady income with less risk than equity-based investments like stocks or ETFs. Examples include government bonds, corporate bonds, Public Provident Fund (PPF), National Savings Certificate (NSC), Kisan Vikas Patra (KVP), Sukanya Samriddhi Yojana (SSY) and fixed deposits.

3. Mutual funds

Mutual funds provide an easy and accessible way for small investors to gain exposure to various markets, with diversity of exposure too. Mutual funds offer investors multiple investments at once through one portfolio, which could include stocks, bonds or any combination thereof. Equity-oriented balanced funds can even provide debt exposure!

4. Real estate and REITs

In India, investing in physical properties like residential and commercial real estate is an increasingly common practice. Real estate investments provide both steady cash flow through rent payments as well as potential value appreciation over time.

REITs (real estate investment trusts) are entities that own, operate or finance income-producing real estate properties and allow individual investors to gain exposure to their profits without having to buy commercial real estate directly themselves. REITs are listed entities which primarily invest in office and commercial rental real estate properties like office buildings, shopping malls, apartments and hotels. They provide regular returns to their investors from the rental yields they fetch. Their main advantages are their steady yield, diversification and long-term capital appreciation benefits.

5. Gold/commodities:
Gold has long been seen as a safe haven for investment in India, and many people invest in physical or electronic gold ETFs as a hedge against inflation. Other commodities, like silver and oil, may also be options, but they are less commonly chosen by individual investors.

6. Infrastructure investment trusts (InvITs)

These are similar to REITs, in that they invest in infrastructure projects like highways or power transmission assets rather than real estate. InvITs allow developers of these assets to monetize them more easily by pooling multiple projects under a trust structure. They also pool money from multiple investors and acquire assets, which then generate cash flow over time. Part of this return consists of dividends and the remainder is in the form of capital appreciation.

7. Cash and cash equivalents

These assets include liquid funds, money market funds and savings accounts that offer low returns but great safety and liquidity.

Process for selection of assets

Asset allocation involves choosing how you will divide up your investments among various asset classes such as stocks, bonds, cash or other alternatives. This process plays a pivotal role in shaping both the risk and return profiles of an investment portfolio.

1. Understand your financial goals

Before you begin the asset allocation process, you need to have a clear understanding of your financial goals. These goals could be short-term (like saving for a vacation or a down payment on a car), medium-term (like saving for a down payment on a house), or long-term (like saving for retirement or your child's education). Your financial goals will greatly influence your choice of asset allocation.

2. Determine your risk tolerance

Risk tolerance refers to your ability and willingness to tolerate fluctuations in investment returns over time, and this varies from individual to individual. Usually, investments that bring higher potential returns carry more significant risks. An aggressive investor might prefer to invest in equity funds while a conservative investor might lean more towards bonds or fixed-income securities as investments.

3. Identify your investment horizon

Your investment horizon is integral to your asset allocation decisions. Essentially, the longer the time horizon, the more the risk-taking that is possible, given the additional time for recovery should any unexpected losses arise.

4. Consider your liquidity needs

If you anticipate that you may quickly need to access funds, such as for short-term needs, more liquid investments (cash or money market funds) might be best for you.

5. Analyse the market conditions

Your financial goals, risk tolerance and investment horizon should ultimately drive your asset allocation decisions; however, current economic and market conditions could play an influential role too.

After considering all these variables, you can create an asset allocation ratio that best meets your needs. For instance, young investors saving towards retirement might allocate 70 per cent of their investments to equities, 20 per cent to bonds and 10 per cent to cash instruments, while retired investors looking to protect their capital might opt to invest 30 per cent of their funds in equities, 50 per cent in bonds and 20 per cent in cash instruments.

Once your asset allocation break-up is done, it's essential that your portfolio be periodically adjusted in order to stay in line with it. Rebalancing often entails the selling of assets that have performed particularly well (which now make up more of your portfolio) while purchasing more of the underperforming ones (which now represent smaller percentages of your portfolio).

Remember, asset allocation can vary significantly based on individual circumstances. To make sure your allocation meets your unique circumstances effectively and safely, consulting a financial adviser could prove useful for you.

Selection of debt investments

Debt investments (also referred to as fixed-income securities) are an asset class that offers returns in the form of periodic fixed payments with eventual principal returns at maturity. They typically consist of government and corporate bonds, certificates of deposit and fixed deposits; all are considered relatively lower-risk investments suitable for investors looking for short-term financial goals or stable monthly returns.

Case study: Sunita Patil—Selection of Debt Investments

Background

Sunita Patil, a forty-year-old Pune-based schoolteacher has managed to save some of her earnings of over fifteen years for future expenses like tuition fees for her son's engineering college course and related costs. Sunita will require around Rs 10 lakh over five years for the tuition fees, which will soon become due, at the institution where her son now studies.

Sunita decides that her financial goal and risk tolerance should dictate her investments. She chooses various debt instruments offered by banks with guaranteed returns that are protected up to Rs 5 lakh per depositor per bank by the Deposit Insurance and Credit Guarantee Corporation (DICGC).

Sunita also invests in debt mutual funds, which invest in bonds and fixed-income securities. Debt mutual funds offer higher potential returns than fixed deposits. However, their higher risk requires careful management. She chooses funds that invest in high-quality bonds and earn decent returns. Sunita acknowledges the impact that interest rates can have on these returns. When interest rates increase, bond prices fall, and when interest rates decrease, bond prices rise. However, Sunita believes that debt instruments offer safe yet steady returns that best suit her financial goals.

Sunita monitors her debt investments over five years and makes adjustments accordingly, such as changing funds when necessary. If one fund consistently underperforms, Sunita switches it out for one that offers better returns.

Selection of equity investments

Equity investments involve the purchase of shares in a corporation to obtain rights over its assets and profits, giving the investor claims on part of them. While equity investments offer high long-term returns, their higher risk threshold means they should only be undertaken by those with adequate risk tolerance and long-term goals in mind.

There are various approaches to equity investment; an investor can purchase shares directly in either an initial public offering (IPO), from the secondary market through stock exchanges like the NSE or BSE, through equity mutual funds, through Portfolio Management Services (PMS), through the Alternative Investment Funds (AIF) routes, or even take professional help in managing his own equity portfolio.

Equity mutual funds invest primarily in stocks. They may further be divided into various categories, depending on factors like company market capitalization or their investment strategies or other specific themes.

1. **Large-cap funds:** These equity mutual funds invest primarily in large, well-established companies and

therefore tend to be relatively less risky and more stable compared with mid- and small-cap funds.

2. **Mid-cap funds:** These funds invest in companies with medium market caps. These companies may present greater potential for high growth than large caps but also carry greater risks when compared with large-cap funds.

3. **Small-cap funds:** Small-cap funds invest in smaller market-cap companies with high potential returns, should those businesses perform as anticipated. Although high-risk, such investments have the possibility of producing excellent results if the companies invested in perform as predicted.

4. **Multi-cap funds:** Multi-cap funds provide investors with a balance of risk and return, providing flexible asset allocation according to the changing market conditions. Fund managers may make adjustments as necessary.

5. **Equity-linked savings scheme funds (ELSS funds):** These funds provide tax advantages through investments made predominantly in shares and are eligible for tax deduction under Section 80C of the Income-tax Act.

6. **Sector funds:** These funds invest exclusively in one economic sector such as IT, pharma or banking. They carry higher risk owing to their lack of diversification but have the potential to make high returns if their chosen sector performs well.

7. **Thematic funds:** These types of investments focus on investing in specific themes or trends, such as emerging consumer behaviours or ESG (environmental, social and governance). Depending on its chosen focus area, multiple sectors could be represented in these funds' portfolios.

8. **Focused funds:** These funds specialize in selecting up to thirty stocks (typically) for investment, whether across market capitalizations or within specific segments.

9. **Value funds:** These funds employ an investment approach known as value investing, investing in stocks that their fund manager feels are undervalued by the market.

10. **Dividend-yield funds:** These funds invest in companies that regularly pay out dividends, thus aiming to provide the investor with a steady income stream through dividend distribution.

11. **Growth funds:** Growth funds provide investors with exposure to companies expected to experience above-average rates of growth in the market.

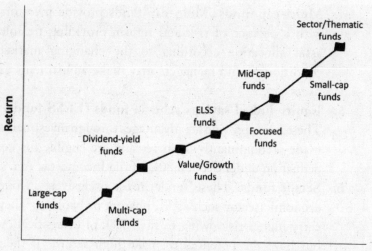

Case study: Rohit Hegde—Selection of Equity Investments

Background

Rohit Hegde, a thirty-year-old software engineer living in Bengaluru, has been employed at a multinational corporation for eight years. He earns a healthy salary and enjoys a comfortable lifestyle. But Rohit recognizes the need to start saving and investing for the future, especially in the matter of retirement.

Rohit decides, after conducting extensive research and consulting a financial adviser, to invest in equity. Although short-term volatility might make equities seem risky and not worth the potential long-term returns they could bring, Rohit appreciates the compounding opportunities offered by the long-term growth potential of equity investments.

Rohit begins his investing by selecting stocks across numerous sectors, such as technology, healthcare and consumer goods, from among large-cap, mid-cap and small-cap companies. This diversification spreads his risk since each category of stocks can perform differently during times of significant developments.

Rohit invests both in individual stocks as well as in equity mutual funds which invest in a portfolio of stocks and are handled by professional fund managers. He opts for both actively and passively managed funds such as index funds, together aimed at outpacing market returns. Rohit maintains patience and discipline in his investing.

Rohit realizes the stock market can be highly unpredictable in the short term, with prices fluctuating depending on various factors, including company performance, economic conditions, political developments and investor sentiment. Yet, he believes in the long-term potential of equity investments and remains committed during market downturns too.

Rohit uses the systematic investment plan (SIP) approach when it comes to investing in mutual funds and makes regular withdrawals from his bank account for the purpose. Not only is this regular investment beneficial but it also allows for cost averaging. When prices decline, more units can be purchased and vice versa.

Rohit meticulously manages his equity investments over the years and makes adjustments as required. Rebalancing of his portfolio to stay aligned with his desired asset allocation is also done frequently, and failing funds are replaced with better-performing funds or removed altogether if they consistently underperform the benchmarks.

Rohit's disciplined equity investing enables him to accumulate an ample retirement corpus that will provide him security during his golden years.

Other investment alternatives

Investing in equities in India can be a complex task, and many investors rely on professional help to navigate the process. You can choose to do this through portfolio management services (PMS), financial advisers or alternative investment funds (AIF). Here is how each of these options can assist you in investing:

1. Portfolio management services (PMS)

- If you avail of PMS, your stocks will be handled by a professional portfolio manager who will make investment decisions based on your financial goals and risk tolerance. This is suitable for high-net-worth individuals as the minimum investment is usually quite high, often starting at Rs 50 lakh.
- The portfolio manager makes all the buying and selling decisions, keeping in mind your investment objectives. The portfolio is customized according to your needs.
- In PMS, you own individual shares, and hence the taxation will be based on your holding period (short-term or long-term capital gains tax).
- Make sure to check the track record, management fees and tax implications before choosing a PMS provider.

2. Financial advisers

- These professionals help you plan your investments based on your financial goals and risk tolerance.

They provide advice on various investment avenues, including equities, bonds, mutual funds, insurance and more.

- Financial advisers can be individuals or firms and are usually paid a fee for their services. Some advisers are also paid a commission by the companies whose products they sell, so make sure to clarify this beforehand.
- The Securities and Exchange Board of India (SEBI) has regulations in place for financial advisers, so ensure that your adviser is registered with SEBI before you hire the person or firm.

3. Alternative investment funds (AIF)

- AIFs are funds established or incorporated in India for the purpose of pooling in capital from Indian and foreign investors for investing as per a pre-decided policy.
- AIFs can invest in equities, debt, real estate, commodities and even unlisted securities. They are classified into three categories by SEBI: Categories I, II and III. Category-III AIFs are allowed to invest in listed equities.
- AIFs are typically for sophisticated or institutional investors as they have a high minimum investment requirement, often in crores of rupees.
- AIFs can offer unique strategies and investments not available through traditional mutual funds. But they are also less regulated than mutual funds, so they are potentially a higher-risk avenue through which to invest.

Regardless of the route you choose, remember that investment in equities always has its risks. Always do thorough research and consult with a trusted financial adviser before making any investment decisions. Additionally, remember to diversify your investments to spread and mitigate the risks.

Selection of mutual funds

Indian investors have access to many types of mutual funds; here is an outline of some key ones:

1. **Equity funds:** These mutual funds invest in shares of various companies. They can be further categorized into large-cap funds, mid-cap funds, small-cap funds and sector funds for easy classification.

2. **Debt funds:** These invest in debt instruments such as government bonds, treasury bills, corporate bonds and other fixed-income investments, such as government securities or municipal bonds. These funds can also further be subdivided into short-term, medium-term and long-term categories, each of which accommodates different investment goals and time horizons.

3. **Money market funds:** These funds invest in highly liquid and short-term instruments such as treasury bills or commercial papers and are generally perceived as offering more security but lower returns.

4. **Balanced or hybrid funds:** These invest in both equity and debt securities to achieve optimal risk-return profiles, typically using equity-oriented hybrid funds for equity exposure or debt-oriented hybrid funds for debt exposure.

5. **Index funds:** Index funds track specific indexes like the Sensex or Nifty to replicate their performance and aim at providing comparable returns to investors.

6. **Sector funds:** These funds invest in specific sectors of the economy, such as IT, pharma or FMCG. Sector funds often offer higher returns with limited diversification risks involved, and the returns could prove to be higher than those from standard mutual funds.

7. **Equity-linked savings schemes (ELSS):** These schemes are tax-saving mutual funds which invest mainly in

equities. Investments made in ELSS funds qualify for deduction under Section 80C of the Income-tax Act.

8. **Fund of funds (FoFs):** These mutual funds invest in other mutual funds run by different asset management companies (AMCs).

9. **Thematic funds:** These investments target companies that fit particular themes or trends (for instance, emerging consumer trends or clean energy).

10. **International/global funds:** These funds invest in stocks or equity-related securities of companies listed outside India.

11. **Gold funds:** Gold funds invest directly or through ETFs in gold-related assets and securities.

Each of these categories represents different asset classes that investors can diversify into. Individuals should seek the advice of a financial planner on selecting appropriate mutual funds to match their asset allocation.

Selection of real estate investments and REITs

Real estate investment refers to the purchase of properties for rental income or for potential capital-appreciation purposes, either of which could provide diversification benefits not found with stocks and bonds. Yet, investing in this form of tangible asset requires significant capital as property markets may vary widely, depending on factors like economic conditions, interest rates and location.

Case study: Arjun Iyer—Selection of Real Estate Investments

Background

Arjun Iyer, a forty-five-year-old accomplished businessman living in Delhi, has amassed significant wealth. Yet, most of it had been sitting idle in his bank account, earning only minimal interest over time. Recently he has decided to put his wealth to better use by investing it instead.

After conducting extensive research into various investment options, Arjun decides to put his money into real estate. He knows the property market in Delhi offers strong growth potential due to increasing urbanization and housing demand. Ownership of property can bring steady rental income streams too!

Arjun devotes a lot of time and effort to researching the property market. He studies property prices across different locations, rental yields and the potential for capital appreciation of various rental units. He also consults a real estate agent and a lawyer about the legal considerations in the matter of ownership of properties bought as investments.

Arjun ultimately purchases a property in a prime location in Delhi, which he rents out to an established company for regular rental income, and which will increase his wealth over time through price appreciation too.

Arjun also invests in real estate investment trusts (REITs), which are companies that own or finance income-producing real estate properties.

REITs offer investors a way to profit from real estate ownership without actually purchasing properties themselves. There are four major REITs operating in India, as of 2023:

- Embassy Office Parks REIT (Embassy), which launched India's first REIT in April 2019
- Mindspace REIT, which was launched in June 2020
- Brookfield India Real Estate, launched in February 2021
- Nexus Select Trust REIT, launched in May 2023

Selection of InvITs

Investors seeking to allocate assets in InvITs should carefully consider their various key elements. The evaluation process described below will allow investors to assess the potential returns, risks and overall compatibility of InvITs in their portfolio:

1. **Asset quality:** Look at the underlying assets of the InvIT. These could include highways, power transmission lines, gas pipelines, etc. It's important to understand the quality and revenue-generation capabilities of these assets. The location, operational efficiency and projected life span of these infrastructure projects should also be considered.

2. **Sponsor and manager quality:** An InvIT's sponsor is responsible for setting it up while its manager oversees its daily operations. You should assess their track record, operational efficiency, management quality and reputation in the market, as this will give you an understanding of their ability to guide a trust that can generate steady returns.

3. **Revenue model:** Evaluate the revenue model of the InvIT. Some may generate income based on usage (toll roads, for instance), while others utilize fixed payment models (leasing agreements for telecom towers, for instance). The revenue model of an InvIT plays an integral part in providing predictability and stability to returns from it over time.

4. **Distribution of cash flow:** InvITs must distribute an ample portion of their cash flow back to investors as distribution yield (annual distribution divided by market price), potentially offering ongoing income streams to shareholders.

5. **Valuations:** Just as with any other investment, price matters when it comes to selecting an InvIT for investment. Consider its asset value, the income it generates and other parameters when deciding what price point might make sense for you. Additionally, check

the InvIT's market price as an indicator of its capital-appreciation potential.

6. **Leveraging:** Assess an InvIT's debt levels carefully as excessive borrowing increases risk. SEBI regulations limit InvIT leverage, but this remains an important consideration when investing.

7. **Risk considerations:** Be wary of potential threats such as regulatory changes, the demand risks for infrastructure assets and the operational hazards that could threaten their operations and profits.

8. **Liquidity:** If InvIT units are publicly traded, take note of their trading volume; investments that lack liquidity could become difficult or impossible to sell when necessary.

InvITs are an appealing option when it comes to investing in infrastructure projects with income and diversification potential, yet they also present some risks. It is crucial that investors thoroughly comprehend these risks before proceeding with their InvIT investment decisions or consult a financial adviser or conduct extensive due diligence before making their final decisions.

Publicly traded InvITs: Certain InvITs can be publicly listed and traded on the stock exchanges, like shares of any company, giving investors access to secondary market units of these InvITs for purchase and sale.

The key listed InvITs in India are:

- IRB InvIT Fund is the first InvIT in the highway sector and was launched in 2017
- India Grid Trust is the largest InvIT in the power transmission sector and was launched in 2017
- PowerGrid Infrastructure Investment Trust is also in the power transmission sector and was launched in 2021

Selection of gold investments

Gold has long been used as both an asset to store and a form of currency, providing investors with a way to hedge against inflation or currency fluctuations and functioning as an investment safe haven during times of political unrest. By investing in gold you could build long-term security while protecting yourself in times of turmoil or economic distress.

Case study: Meena Iyengar—Selection of Gold Investments

Background

Meena Iyengar, a thirty-five-year-old homemaker living in Chennai, is making arrangements for her daughter's wedding, which is several years away. In Indian culture, gold is not only part of the wedding ceremony but is also passed on from generation to generation as wealth. Meena plans on purchasing a significant amount of it before this important event in her daughter's life.

Meena opts to invest in gold through exchange-traded funds (ETFs), which track the price of the metal on an exchange and will allow her to gradually accumulate an impressive stash for her daughter's marriage. Each month, Meena purchases small quantities through this strategy, which is somewhat similar to the systematic mutual fund plans. Eventually, she'll amass a good quantity of gold to gift to her daughter.

Gold ETFs offer many advantages over physical gold, such as in the matter of storage, security and purity. Furthermore, these ETFs may be purchased and sold at any time during market hours at their prevailing market price, providing investors their much-needed liquidity.

Meena also considers investing in sovereign gold bonds (SGBs), issued by the Government of India, which are denominated in grams of gold, fetch a fixed interest rate and also appreciate in price over eight years, with exit options available from year five. These bonds appear well aligned with Meena's financial goals.

By investing in gold, Meena not only fulfils her specific goal of buying gold for her daughter's wedding but is also hedging against inflation and currency risk.

In the case of each asset class—debt, equity, real estate and gold—the choice of investment for an individual will depend on several factors, including the individual's financial goals, risk tolerance, investment horizon and personal preferences.

For Sunita, the schoolteacher who needed funds for her son's education, debt instruments provided the safety and stability she needed. For Rohit, the software engineer planning for his retirement, equity investments offered him the potential to get high returns over the long term. For Arjun, the businessman who wanted to earn rental income and capitalize on property appreciation, real estate was the preferred choice. And for Meena, the homemaker saving for her daughter's wedding, investing in gold instruments was the best way to accumulate the precious metal over time.

However, diversification across asset classes should always be at the core of one's investment strategy. By putting money in an array of asset classes, the risks are reduced and there is potential enhancement of your returns. Your mix of investments would be based on your individual circumstances, so it is advisable to seek assistance from an adviser prior to making your decision on what it should be.

Attainment of financial goals calls for careful planning and disciplined investing. By understanding the various asset classes that exist and by selecting from them those that align with your goals and risk tolerance, a robust long-term financial plan can be created, which will serve you well in the short and long term.

Chapter 9

Execute Your Portfolio

Equity investment platforms

With so many investment platforms in India available today, investors have ample chances to grow their wealth and achieve their financial objectives. Investors can decide how best they wish to expand their wealth and achieve financial security by selecting platforms suited to their risk appetite, investment horizon and financial goals. Here are some prominent platforms you can use for investing.

1. National Stock Exchange (NSE) and Bombay Stock Exchange (BSE)

These are the two major stock exchanges in India offering various investment instruments. They are platforms that offer stock, derivative and securities trading through registered brokers. They provide investors with transparent trading environments where they can take part in the corporate growth of well-known firms as well as invest in promising start-ups. Their registered brokers act as mediators between investors and the markets.

2. Mutual funds

Mutual funds offer individuals an easy and professional way to diversify their investments using professional fund management services, making diversified investments simpler for them. Their platforms streamline the investment process and offer investors access to various mutual funds from various asset management companies, giving them a great choice of funds suited to their objectives and risk profiles. Investors may choose from among equity funds, debt funds, hybrid funds or sector-specific funds, depending on their preferences and risk profile. Mutual fund platforms provide investors with a user-friendly environment in which to explore and invest in funds, monitor their portfolio performance and redeem their investments efficiently and conveniently. Popular Indian platforms used for mutual fund investments include Mutual Fund Utilities (MFU), CAMS Online, Karvy Online, Groww, Paytm Money and Zerodha Coin.

3. Robo-advisory platforms

In recent years, robo-advisory platforms have grown increasingly popular. Leveraging sophisticated algorithms and data analysis techniques, these platforms offer personalized investment advice tailored to individual risk profiles, financial goals and investment horizons. Robo-advisory platforms make investing easier, particularly for individuals without extensive financial knowledge. Investors can create accounts on these platforms, answer a series of questions designed to assess their risk profile and financial goals and receive tailored investment recommendations based on them. Robo-advisory platforms typically provide investors with a diversified portfolio of mutual funds or ETFs, tailored specifically for them based on their risk profile. Scripbox, Kuvera, Goalwise and ET Money are some of the popular examples in India.

4. Online discount brokerages

These outfits have revolutionized the way individuals invest in stocks, mutual funds, commodities and other financial instruments. Offering lower brokerage fees than traditional brokers, these brokerages have made investing more cost-effective for people. Investors can execute trades online, gain access to research tools such as the Bloomberg terminal and monitor portfolios in real time with these user-friendly platforms that provide educational resources as well as customer support to aid customers on their investment journeys. Some of the well-known online discount brokerages in India are Zerodha, Upstox, 5paisa and Angel Broking.

5. National Pension System (NPS)

This scheme is an opt-in retirement savings account run by the Pension Fund Regulatory and Development Authority. Individuals can invest their savings in it to build a fund for their retirement days. NPS provides investors with various investment options, including equity, corporate bonds and government securities. Investors may make contributions via authorized intermediaries such as banks and mutual fund companies. NPS provides tax benefits under Section 80CCD of the Income-tax Act, making it a highly attractive retirement savings solution. Once retirement approaches, the funds in one's NPS may be converted to purchase an annuity, which will provide the investor with a regular income stream.

Platforms for debt instruments

1. Fixed Deposits (FDs)

In India, these have long been a go-to investment option, especially among conservative investors seeking steady returns.

Offered by both banks and non-banking financial companies (NBFCs), FDs require investors to put in a fixed sum over an agreed term at an established interest rate, typically higher than savings account rates. FDs provide capital protection with predictable returns over several months or years and include either regular payouts of interest or full payout upon maturity.

2. Public Provident Fund (PPF)

The Public Provident Fund is an affordable long-term savings scheme offered by the Indian government. It offers attractive interest rates. Investors can open a PPF account at any nationalized bank or post office, make regular contributions over fifteen years and build an impressive corpus over time. These contributions are eligible for tax deduction under Section 80C of the Income-tax Act. The lock-in period of fifteen years adds to one's discipline of saving. The interest rates are set and revised periodically by the government authorities.

3. National Stock Exchange debt market

The National Stock Exchange (NSE) has the NSE debt market, where investors can buy and sell various debt instruments such as government bonds, corporate bonds, debentures and treasury bills. Primary issuances as well as secondary market trading in these debt instruments are available via this dedicated platform, which operates transparently yet reliably, allowing investors to trade debt instruments easily and reliably.

4. Bombay Stock Exchange debt market

As with the National Stock Exchange (NSE), the Bombay Stock Exchange's (BSE's) debt segment offers investors a platform for trading in debt instruments, including government and corporate bonds, commercial papers and certificates of deposit. The transparent and efficient trading system enables customers to gain access to a more expansive selection of options on offer at BSE than at NSE.

5. The electronic debt bidding platform (EBP)

The EBP is an initiative of the Reserve Bank of India to facilitate the sale of government bonds and treasury bills through primary market auctions. Retail investors may participate in the auctions by placing bids for specific securities. The bidders then wait for the auction results to receive the allocations. The EBP provides investors with an accessible means of investing in government debt securities in India.

6. Fixed Income Money Market and Derivatives Association of India (FIMMDA)

FIMMDA is India's industry association which advocates for the growth and development of fixed-income markets. It operates an electronic trading platform known as F-TRAC (Fixed Income Trading and Reporting System), which allows participants to trade in various debt instruments electronically. These instruments could be government bonds, corporate bonds, commercial papers and treasury bills. The trading of debt securities is electronic and the platform functions as a central price discovery and trading hub.

7. Bond-issuing companies and financial institutions in India

There are various companies and financial institutions in India offering direct investment opportunities in their debt instruments like bonds or debentures issued for the purpose of their operation or expansion. Primary issuances of these bonds are open for direct participation by investors. The details regarding bond offerings by these institutions can be obtained from their respective websites, from the stock exchanges or the financial newspapers.

Please be aware that these platforms' availability and features may change over time. To stay informed on this matter, it is advisable to visit their respective websites directly or seek the advice of financial professionals for the latest details.

Platforms for gold investments

Investing in gold has been a long-standing tradition in India, given its cultural and economic significance. In recent years, there has been an increasing interest in gold investments as a means of diversifying one's portfolio and safeguarding against market volatility. Luckily, there are several platforms available in India that cater to individuals looking to invest in gold. Let's explore these platforms in more detail:

1. Gold exchange-traded funds (ETFs)

Gold ETFs have gained in popularity as a convenient and cost-effective way to invest in gold. These funds are listed on the stock exchanges and trade like stocks. Gold ETFs aim to track gold prices, allowing investors to gain exposure to gold without physically owning the metal. Each unit of a gold ETF represents a specific quantity of gold. The units can be bought and sold through stockbrokers on the exchange. Gold ETFs provide liquidity and transparency and eliminate the need for storage and the security concerns associated with owning physical gold. Popular gold ETFs in India are HDFC Gold ETF, SBI Gold ETF and ICICI Prudential Gold ETF.

2. Sovereign gold bonds (SGBs)

SGBs are government-issued securities denominated in grams of gold. These bonds provide individuals the opportunity to invest in gold in a paperless form. SGBs have a specified tenure and pay interest semi-annually. At maturity, investors receive the equivalent value of the bond in cash, based on the prevailing gold prices. SGBs offer the dual benefit of price appreciation and interest income. These bonds are issued periodically by the Reserve Bank of India (RBI) on behalf of the Government of India. Investors can purchase SGBs through designated banks or authorized stockbrokers during the issuance period. SGBs provide a secure and regulated investment option for those looking to invest in gold for the long term.

3. Gold savings accounts

These accounts are offered by various banks and financial institutions and allow investors to buy and sell gold in electronic form. These accounts provide the flexibility of investing in gold in smaller denominations and offer convenience and ease of transaction. Investors can purchase gold in the form of units, which are held in their accounts. The gold can be redeemed in physical form or converted into cash, as per the investor's preference. Banks like HDFC Bank, ICICI Bank and Kotak Mahindra Bank offer gold savings accounts to their customers, providing them a reliable and secure platform for investing in gold.

4. Digital gold platforms

Digital gold platforms have gained in popularity due to their accessibility and ease of use. These platforms allow investors to buy and hold gold in digital form. They partner with trusted gold refiners to offer gold of assured purity. Investors can purchase gold in small denominations, such as in grams or even fractions of grams, as per their investment capacity. The purchased gold is securely stored in vaults on their behalf. Digital gold platforms also offer investors the facility to sell their gold and redeem it for cash. Some of the popular digital gold platforms in India are Paytm Gold, PhonePe Gold and Google Pay Gold. These platforms have simplified the process of investing in gold and have made it accessible to a wider range of investors.

5. Gold accumulation plans (GAPs)

These plans, also referred to as gold savings schemes, are offered by jewellers and financial institutions in India. They enable investors to accumulate gold gradually over a period of time by making regular monthly contributions. The accumulated contributions are used to purchase gold at the prevailing market rates. At the end of the tenure, investors can either take physical delivery of the accumulated gold or receive the equivalent value in cash. GAPs allow for a disciplined approach to investing in gold and can be an attractive option for individuals who prefer a systematic investment strategy.

6. Gold jewellery retailers

Investing in physical gold in the form of gold jewellery or gold coins is a traditional and widely practised method of saving in India. Gold jewellery retailers offer a wide range of gold jewellery designs and gold coins of varying weights. Purchase of gold from trusted retailers ensures the authenticity and purity of the metal. It is important to look for hallmarked jewellery and proper certifications to ensure the quality of the gold. Investing in physical gold provides one the advantage of owning a tangible asset that can be worn or stored securely.

It is important to note that investing in gold, like investing in anything else, carries risks. The price of gold can be volatile, and investors should carefully consider their investment objectives, risk tolerance and time horizon before investing. Conducting thorough research, understanding the costs and charges associated with each platform and seeking professional advice can help individuals make informed decisions when it comes to investing in gold.

In conclusion, the availability of various platforms in India has made gold more accessible and convenient for individuals to invest in. Whether through gold ETFs, sovereign gold bonds, gold savings accounts, digital gold platforms, gold accumulation plans or acquisition of physical gold from jewellery retailers, investors have a range of options to choose from. Each platform has its own advantages in terms of liquidity, ease of transaction and storage. By selecting the most suitable platform based on their personal preferences and due diligence, investors can participate in the gold market and potentially benefit from gold price appreciation over time.

Before investing in gold through any platform, it is crucial to conduct thorough research and understand the features, charges and risks associated with each option. Investors should evaluate factors such as historical performance, fund manager expertise, expense ratios and investment strategies before making their investment decisions. It is also important to assess one's risk tolerance and investment goals to align one's investments with one's individual financial objectives. A financial adviser can provide valuable insights and help investors select the most suitable platforms for their individual needs.

In conclusion, the Indian investment landscape offers a wide range of platforms catering to diverse investment preferences. Whether it's stocks, mutual funds, fixed deposits, retirement schemes or real estate, individuals in India have numerous avenues for growing their wealth and achieving their financial aspirations. It is essential to approach investments with a well-defined strategy, consider the risk factors and stay informed about market trends to make informed investment decisions.

By leveraging the available investment platforms effectively, investors can embark on their journey towards long-term financial growth and security.

Platforms for Real Estate

Real estate crowdfunding platforms

Crowdfunding has emerged as an attractive investment option in India, providing investors with a means by which to participate in real-estate projects for smaller investment amounts. There are various crowdfunding platforms available today. They enable individuals to benefit from investing in real estate, which would otherwise require significant up-front capital investment, by pooling contributions from many investors. Investors can diversify their portfolios by incorporating residential, commercial and industrial property investments to generate returns through rental income or appreciation of these properties. Real estate crowdfunding platforms provide investors with detailed information on projects, including their location, the expected returns from them and the risk factors. Investors can evaluate these opportunities based on their preferences and risk tolerance. Examples in India of such platforms include PropShare, SmartOwner and Assetmonk.

Chapter 10

Tracking Investments

Tracking investments is essential to managing a portfolio and reaching one's financial goals; it keeps one informed and makes one capable of performance analysis and of making strategy adjustments as needed. Here's our comprehensive guide to tracking investments in India and the tools and techniques one may use for efficient tracking:

1. Establish an investment tracking system

First, develop a reliable system to keep an eye on your investments. This could range from spreadsheets or more sophisticated tracking software programs. The key here is to have one central place where you can record and update your investment details regularly. You must be able to key in your purchase date, cost, current value as well as income or dividends received. You must make regular adjustments as your portfolio changes over time.

2. Portfolio tracking tools in India

Take advantage of the online portfolio tracking tools available in India to simplify the tracking of your portfolio investments. These tools offer real-time price updates, performance analysis and customizable reports. Here are some popular tracking platforms in India:

a) **Moneycontrol Portfolio Manager:** This tool offers an advanced portfolio tracking feature which makes the management of investments simple; it provides real-time updates and news alerts as well as customizable charts to analyse your portfolio's performance.

b) **Groww:** Groww is an investment platform with an easy portfolio tracking feature, enabling you to invest across different asset classes like stocks and mutual funds while receiving regular portfolio updates from its experts. It also features detailed insights, investment analysis tools and regular portfolio updates so your portfolio remains up-to-date at all times!

c) **ET Money** is an award-winning financial app offering portfolio tracking services. You can sync all your investments, track their performance and receive tailored advice based on your portfolio and financial goals.

3. Brokerage and trading platforms

For those investing in stocks, take advantage of the portfolio tracking features offered on brokerage and trading platforms like Zerodha, ICICI Direct, HDFC Securities, etc., to monitor your stock holdings, view performance charts and receive market updates. Further, many platforms also provide comprehensive reports, trade-history records and analytic tools, enabling you to track your investments effectively.

4. Mutual fund tracking

For tracking mutual fund investments, here are the options:

a) **Asset management company (AMC) websites**: Most mutual fund houses have their own websites offering detailed information about the funds under management. By signing into your account on one of the respective AMC websites, you can track your mutual fund investments. The websites track the net asset value (NAV) of your funds, their historical performance information and fund factsheets as well as portfolio holdings and more!

b) **Mutual fund aggregator platforms**: Groww, Paisabazaar and Value Research Online are mutual fund aggregator platforms that make it easy to keep an eye on all your investments in mutual funds of various AMCs in one location. These platforms also provide you with fund performance analysis and give you recommendations that will help you make informed investment decisions.

5. Economic and financial news

Staying abreast of economic and financial developments is crucial to understanding the market and its effects on your investments. Follow reliable websites, business channels and newspapers covering the Indian financial markets. Some of them are Moneycontrol, Livemint *Economic Times* and CNBC TV18. They offer in-depth coverage of financial news and also expert analyses of market trends, economic indicators and regulatory changes.

6. Schedule regular analysis of investment statements and broker reports

It is essential that you regularly analyse your investment statements, account statements and the brokerage reports provided by financial institutions or brokers in order to track the performance of your investments, identify any discrepancies and stay informed about matters like dividend payments and expenses as well as fees charged against your portfolio in line with its goals and expenses. Regular review of these documents ensures you remain up to date.

7. Performance evaluation

Briskly track how your investments compare against your goals by reviewing the returns, the risk-adjusted performance and the potential for loss or gain over time.

Such an evaluation will enable you to easily compare your investments with the relevant benchmarks or indices, identify the underperforming items in your portfolio and determine if any adjustments or rebalancing need to be made. Keep track of your objectives, time horizon and risk tolerance to make informed decisions on what investments will suit you best.

8. Seek professional advice

For complex investments that require expert knowledge and advice, consult a financial adviser or investment professional for personalized guidance tailored to your financial goals, risk tolerance and investment horizon. A financial adviser will help you create an investment strategy, track your investments and make sound decisions aligned with your objectives.

9. Reassess your investment strategy and portfolio allocation

On an ongoing basis, revisit your investment strategy and portfolio allocation in line with the changing market dynamics and goals. Regularly assess your portfolio to ensure that it stays aligned with changing requirements while mitigating risks effectively. It will also serve to help optimize your returns.

The effective tracking of investments over time and staying informed are considered among the more challenging elements of investment management. Utilize the tools, platforms and resources available in India to effectively keep tabs on your investments while staying updated about them to achieve your financial goals.

Key takeaways from this section

1. Create a budget by projecting your income and expenses
2. Understand your savings potential based on the budget
3. Finalize your goals based on your priorities and savings
4. Allocate your ASSETs, based on your goals and risk profile
5. Choose the right DEBT products based on your goals
6. Choose the right EQUITY products, including mutual funds, based on your goals
7. Diversify your investments by investing in gold, REITs, InvITs, etc., based on your goals
8. Execute your portfolio using the right platform
9. Track your portfolio regularly

Section 4: Inspect Progress (I)

'Success is the progressive realization of a worthy goal or ideal.'

—Earl Nightingale

Inspecting the progress of a financial plan is crucial in the journey towards financial independence. Regular evaluation allows individuals to track their financial goals, identify areas of improvement and make the necessary adjustments to stay on track. The monitoring of investments and expenses helps one maintain a healthy balance between risk and return, ensuring oneself a secure financial future. As circumstances change, such as due to career shifts or family needs, re-evaluation of one's investment plans becomes essential to adapt to and accommodate these shifts. Also, regular inspection of one's progress fosters discipline, encourages the habit of saving and boosts one's confidence when it comes to financial decision-making.

Chapter 11

Reviewing Financial Plans

Establishing a half-yearly review of your plan can be an excellent way of staying on top of your personal finances and meeting your financial goals. Track your income, expenses, assets and liabilities through this process, and it will help you make better financial decisions and reach your goals quicker than you would otherwise. Here are the steps by which you can create an action plan for review of your investments.

Review IEAL (income, expenses, assets and liabilities)

Step 1: Gather your financial information

Start by collecting all your relevant financial information. This would include:

- Bank statements
- Credit card statements
- Investment statements
- Loan documents
- Loan statements
- Salary slips, business income (if any)
- Insurance policies
- Tax returns

Step 2: Document your income

To accurately account for all sources of income over the past six months—such as salary, business revenue, rental property income or dividends—categorize them by revenue source for clarity.

Step 3: Analyse your expenses

After gathering all the statements from your bank and credit card accounts showing your expenses related to rent/home loan payment/utilities/subscription payments, etc., create an expense list containing all your fixed expenses (rent/home loan payments, etc.,) and your variable expenses (groceries/dining out/entertainment). Doing this will give you a better understanding as to where exactly your money goes each month/year/paycheque period.

Step 4: Review your assets

Your assets could include items such as your home, car, investments and savings accounts, as well as valuable belongings like furniture and artwork. Determine their current value. Review how well your investments have performed over the last six months, and use online resources for property appraisal or consult professional appraisers for this.

Step 5: Evaluate your liabilities

Your liabilities represent everything that you owe—be it home loan payments, student loan balances, car loan instalments to be paid and credit card bills, among many others. Keep track of the outstanding balances under each head to stay aware of where you stand.

Step 6: Calculate your net worth

To determine your net worth, subtract your liabilities from your assets to get an idea of your overall financial health.

This exercise will give you a glimpse of where things stand with regard to money management.

Step 7: Establish your financial goals

Establishing goals will keep you on the path towards financial stability. The goals could range from saving for a vacation, buying a house, paying off debts or setting aside an amount for retirement savings.

Step 8: Establish a revised budget

Based on your income, expenses and goals for the next six months, draft a revised budget that accounts for both fixed and variable costs as well as for money to be set aside in savings accounts.

Step 9: Review your insurance and investments

Carefully review all existing policies to make sure they still fit with your needs, making any required updates as soon as possible. Furthermore, assess whether your portfolio aligns with your current financial goals and risk tolerance in an objective fashion.

Step 10: Schedule your next review

After conducting your review, schedule the next one immediately to keep yourself on track and make adjustments as necessary. Regular reviews allow for faster decision-making processes when the need for them arises and help you adjust your plans as necessary.

Don't expect drastic improvements from one review to the next; what matters is your being aware of your financial standing and taking measures to enhance it.

Reviewing Your Goals

Reviewing your personal finance goals bi-annually is essential to staying on track and making any necessary adjustments to them as time progresses. As circumstances, priorities and needs evolve along your financial journey, regular check-ins allow you to adjust them according to your current circumstances. Here is a detailed process that can be followed for this:

1. Establish your financial goals

Your personal financial goals depend on many different aspects of your lifestyle, your responsibilities, ambitions and personal values. Some common financial goals would be repayment or elimination of debt, saving for retirement, creating an emergency fund, buying a house or investing in wealth creation. To successfully assess and evaluate these goals you must have a firm grasp of both what they mean to you as an individual and why. This understanding should form the cornerstone of the review process.

2. Compile essential information

Before reviewing your goals, gather all the relevant financial information. This would include income details, expense records, investment statements and loan documents. Any additional data relevant to your achievement of financial success should also be accounted for here. Ensure the details provided here are accurate and up to date for a clear view of where you currently stand financially.

3. Evaluate your progress to achieve your goals

Once your goals and data are in order, it's time to assess their progress. Are you on track with reaching your objectives? For instance, if one of your goals involves clearing your debts within a given timeline, take note of where the balance stands at this point in relation to what was originally projected as the balance. Likewise, if saving for a down payment on a house is your aim, then evaluate your savings accounts against the goal amounts and see whether these match up.

Now is also an opportune moment to assess the performance of your investments against particular goals like meeting an expected return rate or expanding to a specific size of portfolio. Check to ensure that your investments are performing according to plan!

4. Analyse and reflect

It is also essential to monitor your progress closely and reflect upon it regularly. If your goals have been achieved or surpassed, take note of what's working well—whether it is your budget planning, your spending discipline, your investments or your additional income streams.

If your goals haven't materialized as planned, try to determine why. Are your expectations too lofty; are unexpected expenses eating into your savings accounts; or are you not making as much as planned or spending more than expected?

5. Make the necessary adjustments

Based on your analysis, adjustments might need to be made, either to your financial habits or to your goals themselves. If your goals are being missed, you may need to find ways to cut expenses, increase your income or alter your investment strategies accordingly.

Sometimes it might be necessary to adapt your goals. For example, if your initial goal was to save Rs 1 lakh in six months' time but you managed only Rs 50,000 in savings, adjustment of either your timeline or the goal amount might be necessary. On the other hand, if your original target has been accomplished, you might consider setting a more ambitious one, going forward.

6. Plan for the upcoming half-year

Utilize your new-found insights from this review to plan for the upcoming half year, such as by updating your budget, setting or revising goals, developing an investment strategy, or devising ways to reduce debt or increase income as necessary.

Conclusion

Remember, reviewing your financial goals should not be seen as an exercise in self-judgement but instead provide you with an accurate picture of where your current finances stand and the steps required for you to move closer towards reaching your goals. Instead, view this process as an invaluable aid on your journey towards your aspirations and values, as something beneficial rather than something in which you pass or fail!

Case study: Suresh Kulkarni—Review of Personal Finance Goals

Background

Suresh Kulkarni is a thirty-five-year-old IT professional living in Mumbai. He lives with his wife, who is a schoolteacher, and their four-year-old daughter. Suresh has set several financial goals at the beginning of the year, which he plans to review on a half-yearly basis. These goals include:

1. Saving Rs 5 lakh for their daughter's future education
2. Reducing credit card debt by Rs 1 lakh
3. Saving Rs 2 lakh for a family vacation abroad
4. Investing Rs 3 lakh in mutual funds

Now, it is time for Suresh's half-yearly financial review.

Step 1: Understanding the financial goals

Suresh and his wife sit down and discuss their goals, reiterating why they have set them and how they aligned with their future plans.

Step 2: Gathering the necessary information

Suresh and his wife collect all the relevant financial documents—bank statements, investment details, credit card statements and income details.

Step 3: Measuring progress made towards goals

They start measuring their progress against each goal:

1. *Saving for daughter's education:* They have saved Rs 2.5 lakh so far, and they are on track.
2. *Reducing credit card debt:* They have managed to reduce the debt by only Rs 50,000, falling short of the goal.
3. *Saving for a vacation:* They have saved Rs 1 lakh and are behind schedule here too.
4. *Investing in mutual funds:* They have invested Rs 1.5 lakh, which is halfway to their original goal.

Step 4: Analysing and reflecting

They review their progress and investigate why certain goals have not been reached as planned. Unexpected medical expenses and higher-than-anticipated inflation have negatively impacted their savings and repayment capabilities. Their investments haven't been yielding the expected returns either, because of market instability.

Step 5: Making the necessary adjustments

Understanding their current situation, Suresh and his wife decide to make a few adjustments:

1. They slightly reduce the vacation savings goal to Rs 1.5 lakh and plan a less expensive holiday.

2. They plan to continue to pare down their credit card debt, even if it might take longer than initially planned.
3. They decide to consult with a financial adviser for better investment strategies to optimize returns from their investments.

Step 6: Planning for the next half-year

Over the following six months, they revise their budget, cutting some discretionary expenses like dining out and entertainment, while prioritizing savings rate increases and debt reduction efforts and reallocating investments based on professional advice. They invest in health insurance policies that will cover unexpected medical costs and investigate ways of saving more for retirement.

Conclusion

Suresh and his wife have recognized that the financial review was not meant to demotivate them but to provide them with an insight into where they stand financially and where they could make the necessary adjustments to stay on track towards their financial goals. They found their biannual review process useful and plan on continuing this practice to stay on course financially.

Reviewing risk

Accounting for risk should always be part of any financial plan. The nature and quantum of risk depend on various factors, like age, income, goals and risk tolerance. Reviewing your plan periodically for risks can ensure that it remains aligned with your personal circumstances. Here is an effective step-by-step process to do just this:

1. Assess your risk tolerance

The first step to understanding your risk tolerance involves understanding the extent of risk you are comfortable taking on.

Would you prefer higher-risk investments that bring potentially higher returns, or safer and less risky investments? Your tolerance could change over time, so it is wise to conduct regular assessments on this aspect of investing.

2. Analyse your asset allocation

Review the asset allocation in your investment portfolio to ascertain where your investments stand today. Are they weighted heavily towards riskier yet higher-return equities? Or have you invested more in bonds which offer safer but lower returns? Is the portfolio diverse across assets, geographies and sectors so as to minimize the risks on these counts? By having such diversification in place, you can mitigate the risk, spreading it across assets and over time.

3. Evaluate the changes in your life circumstances

Any major life change should prompt an assessment of your risk profile, whether that means getting married, having children, buying a house or changing jobs. All these developments could have their effects on how comfortable or risk-tolerant you feel taking on financial liabilities.

4. Outline your financial goals

Take an inventory of your financial goals and their timelines. Longer-term objectives may permit greater risk-taking while short-term goals might demand safer investments.

5. Analyse investment performance

How have your investments performed over the past six months? Investments that consistently underperform or demonstrate high levels of volatility could be riskier than you realize.

6. Examine changes in the market environment

Additionally, it's also vitally important to pay attention to changes in the wider market environment. If the economy enters a recession or volatility increases significantly in your markets, your risk profile might need to be adjusted accordingly.

7. Consult expert opinion

Seeking expert opinion from a financial adviser will also be beneficial in getting you customized guidance tailored specifically for you and helping to explain to you the potential risks that you might encounter in life.

8. Revamp your plan

Once you've evaluated all of these factors, it may be beneficial to revise your financial plan accordingly. Adjustments could involve shifting of the asset allocation, selection of more conservative or aggressive investments, or even revision of your financial goals.

Reviewing for risk is an integral component of developing and maintaining an effective personal financial plan. By conducting regular reviews of your portfolio for risk, you can ensure that your plan continues to align with your risk-tolerance level and financial goals. Keep in mind that managing risks doesn't mean avoiding them entirely; rather, understanding them and making educated decisions is the goal.

Reviewing asset allocation

Asset allocation refers to how your investment capital is distributed among different asset classes such as stocks, bonds, real estate, commodities or cash and equivalents. It aims to balance risk with reward based on the concerned individual's financial goals, risk tolerance levels and time horizon. A review every six months helps to make sure that your asset allocation is in step with your changing financial needs and market trends. Here is how you go about it:

1. Understanding your asset allocation

Asset allocation is a basic investment strategy involving diversifying your investments across asset classes to potentially increase the returns while mitigating the risks. Each class offers differing degrees of risk and returns; stocks tend to experience more gains but carry higher risks, while bonds typically see lower returns with reduced risks. Finding the optimal mix of investments will depend on your goals, tolerance levels and investment time frames.

2. Assess your current asset allocation

The initial step of reviewing your asset allocation should be to gain an understanding of your existing distribution of assets. How much of your portfolio consists of stocks, how much of bonds/fixed income securities/commodities, etc., and what portion is held as cash?

3. Assess your financial goals and risk tolerance

Your asset allocation should reflect both your long-term goals and your risk tolerance. For instance, saving for retirement may warrant greater exposure to equity investments, while saving for shorter goals like down payments on houses might necessitate less risky investments such as bonds or cash held as assets.

Your risk tolerance can fluctuate based on factors like your financial circumstances, age and income, as well as personal preferences. That is why it is crucial that each review period is seen as an opportunity to re-evaluate and update your risk thresholds.

4. Comparing your current allocation with the ideal allocation

After understanding your financial goals and risk tolerance, determine what your optimal asset allocation is. Several rules of thumb can assist you in this, such as '100 minus your age', to estimate equity allocation. But these can only serve as guidelines; your ideal allocation will ultimately depend on your individual circumstances.

Once you've established what your ideal allocation is, compare it with what's been happening so far in terms of reallocation. This will help to determine if any areas need additional attention or whether rebalancing might be required to restore equilibrium to your portfolio.

5. Rebalancing your portfolio

Rebalancing is the practice of realigning the weightages in your portfolio to bring them back in line with what was originally intended. Rebalancing involves the periodic purchase or sale of assets in the portfolio in order to restore the equilibrium between asset groups within it and achieve your original asset allocation plan.

Example: Your ideal portfolio allocation might have been 60 per cent equity and 40 per cent bond investments, but due to the recent stock market strength, it shifted closer to 70 per cent equities and 30 per cent bonds. In such an instance, selling some stocks and purchasing bonds may help return you closer to what was desired.

Rebalancing ensures that your investment strategy remains aligned with both your financial goals and risk tolerance and also acts to get you to 'buy low and sell high'. You can sell a little from the asset classes that have performed exceptionally well and purchase additional units of those that have underperformed.

Conclusion

In summary, reviewing one's asset allocation is an integral component of investment management. Doing this regularly will keep your investments aligned with your desired financial goals while managing the risks within acceptable parameters.

Case study: Ravi Aluri—Reviewing of Asset Allocation

Background

Ravi Aluri is a forty-year-old software engineer living in Hyderabad. He's married and has two children. He has been investing for a decade now, focusing on growing his wealth to secure his children's education and his own retirement. His financial portfolio includes equities, bonds, real estate and cash savings.

At the beginning of the year, Ravi has determined that his ideal asset allocation based on his goals and risk tolerance will be:

- 50 per cent equities
- 30 per cent bonds
- 15 per cent real estate
- 5 per cent cash

1. Assessing current asset allocation

At the half-yearly mark, Ravi and his financial adviser review his portfolio. They calculate the current allocation:

- 60 per cent equities
- 25 per cent bonds
- 10 per cent real estate
- 5 per cent cash

The booming equity markets have inflated the equity portion of Ravi's portfolio.

2. Evaluating financial goals and risk tolerance

Ravi's primary goals remain unaltered—saving for his children's higher education and planning a comfortable retirement. After speaking to his adviser, however, Ravi decides to reduce his risk tolerance slightly, as his children are approaching college-going age. Soon the family would need to liquidate investments for tuition costs. Also, at forty, Ravi wants to gradually shift towards safer assets to secure his retirement corpus.

3. Comparing current and ideal allocations

Ravi's revised ideal allocation, considering his lower risk tolerance, is now:

- 45 per cent equities
- 35 per cent bonds
- 15 per cent real estate
- 5 per cent cash

Comparing this with his current allocation, Ravi realizes he's overweight in equities and underweight in bonds and real estate.

4. Rebalancing the portfolio

Ravi decides that to achieve his ideal allocation, he needs to divest some equity holdings which have given him impressive returns since the recent stock market rally. He sells some at favourable prices and invests the proceeds in bonds and residential real estate, in the hope that both will appreciate over time and the real estate will function as a rental property.

Conclusion

At the conclusion of his review, Ravi's portfolio has been brought closer to its ideal asset allocation. Not only has this exercise helped Ravi in maintaining the diversification he intended to maintain across asset classes, but the diversification is also tailored specifically for his reduced risk tolerance and altered financial goals. Ravi's example illustrates the significance of regular review and rebalancing of one's portfolio to manage risks while staying on course to meet one's financial goals amid changing market conditions. Ravi is now setting an appointment six months hence for another review so his financial journey stays aligned with his evolving needs.

Chapter 12

Updating Goals after the Half-Yearly Review Process

Once you've conducted a half-yearly review of your personal finances, it is time to revise your financial goals accordingly. Your revision should reflect any new insights into the condition of your finances or any successes achieved along the way.

Here are a few steps that should help get you on your way:

1. Assess your progress

Take some time to reflect on how far along the path you are in achieving your original goals, whether it means meeting any of them or finding that some are no longer relevant to you as much as earlier. Your progress report from this review can serve as the blueprint for the future steps you will take.

2. Revamp your financial goals

Based on your current financial status, life circumstances and priorities, re-evaluation of your goals can make sense based on where you stand now. For instance, if debts have been cleared, you could potentially focus more on savings. Or if a promotion has come your way, you can set aside more for your retirement corpus. Or maybe there is someone special in your life you need to save for, such as a child who is going in for higher education.

3. Set priorities in the matter of your financial goals

Your goals might include several financial aspirations. Prioritize them according to importance and urgency, such as saving for retirement over saving for a car.

4. Establish SMART goals

Set financial goals that are specific, measurable, achievable, relevant and time-bound (SMART). Instead of saying, 'I want to save more money,' your goal should be SMART, such as 'I will save Rs 50,000 by December,' if that's your target vacation goal.

5. Make adjustments to your budget

Your financial goals have an immediate effect on your budget, whether that means cutting expenses or increasing income to reach a savings goal faster. Review your budget periodically so it supports these goals.

6. Establish strategies to achieve your goals

Once you've set new financial goals, develop plans to meet them. This may involve selecting appropriate investment vehicles or setting up automatic savings accounts or discovering ways to expand your income sources.

7. Track your progress regularly

Finally, create a schedule to track the progress you are making towards meeting your updated goals on an ongoing basis. Regular reviews can keep you on the path towards meeting them while making adjustments quickly if needed.

Updating your financial goals should not be seen as an annual task; rather, it should be treated as an ongoing process. As life circumstances and finances change, so too must your goals. By periodically reviewing and revising them to stay current with your changing lifestyle demands, aspirations and goals, you ensure your overall financial plan remains relevant and useful in helping to meet them.

Case study: Geeta Prabhu—Updating Financial Goals

Background

Geeta Prabhu, a thirty-two-year-old digital marketing professional, lives in New Delhi. She has been working hard to get ahead in her career and save for her future. She has set several financial goals at the beginning of the year:

1. Save Rs 2 lakh for her upcoming wedding
2. Pay off Rs 1 lakh of her car loan
3. Invest Rs 1.5 lakh in mutual funds
4. Keep an emergency fund of Rs 50,000

Six months later, it's time for Geeta's financial review.

1. Review of progress

Geeta starts by reviewing her progress against her goals:

1. She has managed to save Rs 2.5 lakh for her wedding, surpassing her goal
2. She has made consistent repayments and reduced her car loan to Rs 30,000
3. She has invested Rs 1 lakh in mutual funds, which is less than planned
4. She has Rs 60,000 in her emergency fund, which is more than what she initially aimed for

2. Re-evaluation of financial goals

Geeta has had a few changes in her life circumstances. She has been promoted with a substantial salary increase and is now married. Her husband also works and contributes to the household income.

With her increased income and marital status, Geeta decides to:

1. Start saving for a down payment on a house.
2. Increase her investments in mutual funds.
3. Continue to build her emergency fund.

3. Prioritization of goals

Geeta decides that saving for a house is her top priority, followed by investing more in mutual funds. While she'll continue to build her emergency fund, it's not her primary focus at this time.

4. Setting SMART goals

Next, Geeta sets SMART goals:

1. Save Rs 5 lakh for a house down payment over the next eighteen months
2. Invest an additional Rs 2 lakh in mutual funds over the next year
3. Increase the emergency fund to Rs 1 lakh over the next year

5. Adjustment of budget

Geeta revises her budget in the light of her new goals. She allocates more of her income towards savings and investments while decreasing her discretionary spending, such as on dining out or shopping.

6. Establishing strategies to achieve goals

Geeta implements an automatic monthly transfer from her salary account into her savings and investment accounts in order to consistently save and invest every month. With this approach in place, Geeta ensures she remains disciplined about saving and investing every month.

7. Proactive reviewing of progress

Geeta should schedule regular financial reviews so she can keep an eye on her progress, adjust her plans as necessary and remain on course to meet her financial goals.

Conclusion

Geeta's half-yearly financial review enables her to revise her goals to reflect her current life situation more accurately, providing her with a road map towards reaching them. Geeta's experience exemplifies why financial goals need to be regularly revised in line with life changes, income fluctuations and evolving priorities.

Updating the budget

An effective budget serves as the cornerstone of personal financial management, yet life circumstances, goals, expenses and income sources constantly shift and the budget needs to be adjusted accordingly. Here is a step-by-step process for updation or revision of your budget every six months:

1. Begin by reviewing your current budget

Begin with an in-depth examination of your existing budget. Evaluate your monthly income, fixed expenses (such as rent or home loan payments), variable expenses such as groceries or utility bills, discretionary spending like dining out or entertainment, as well as savings or investments using financial software, spreadsheets or even pen and paper to get a picture of where your money is currently going. It is critical that you first gain an understanding of your current spending habits relative to your financial goals before initiating any changes or making plans or decisions!

2. Assess your income

Take note of any changes in your income since the preparation of the budget. Did you receive an increase or a bonus, start some side hustle, or start an independent side business venture? The budget must reflect these shifts. If your income has increased, consider where the extra cash should go—into savings accounts, investments or debt reduction? Conversely, if income has diminished over time, pinpoint the areas where you can cut your expenses to stay within your means and live sensibly!

3. Evaluate your expenses

Next, evaluate your expenses. Have any fixed costs changed as a result of your having moved or your changing lifestyle? Have variable expenses increased or decreased, or have more non-essentials been spent on than needed? Understanding your expenses is vitally important when updating a budget plan.

4. Consider your financial goals

Spend some time carefully considering all your short- and long-term goals regarding money. Perhaps some goals have been accomplished, such as the paying off of a loan. You might repurpose those funds towards another objective or set a new one, like saving for a down payment on a house, starting a retirement fund or building an emergency reserve. These changes must reflect in your budget as you create it.

5. Adjust your budget

Now that you have evaluated your income, expenses and financial goals, revise your budget accordingly. Allocate portions of your income for different categories of investment or spends that align with your goals while considering fixed and variable costs, also providing some funds for discretionary spending for optimal budget management.

6. Implement and track your budget

Finally, it is time to implement and track your updated budget. Use whatever method suits you best: an app, software or pen and paper. Regularly monitor your spending to make sure it adheres to the budget, as any significant deviations will require further changes or adjustments in the spending categories in your plan.

Updating your budget should not be treated as a one-off activity but as an ongoing review and adjustment process. A budget that flexibly adapts to changes in your financial status, life circumstances and goals is an invaluable asset in managing your personal finances to lead you to financial freedom and security.

Case study: Rohit Deshpande—Updating the Budget

Background

Rohit Deshpande is a twenty-eight-year-old software engineer residing in Pune. At the beginning of the year, he set up a budget to manage his income and expenses. Six months later, it's time for Rohit's financial review and budget update.

1. Review of current budget

Rohit's original monthly budget is as follows:

- Income: Rs 1,00,000
- Rent: Rs 20,000
- Groceries and utilities: Rs 15,000
- Eating out and entertainment: Rs 10,000
- Car loan repayment: Rs 15,000
- Savings and investments: Rs 40,000

2. Reassessment of income

Over the past six months, Rohit has received a promotion with a significant pay raise. His monthly income is now Rs 1,20,000.

3. Evaluation of expenses

Rohit's rent remains the same, but his grocery bills have increased slightly as a result of inflation. He's also been dining out less and spending less on entertainment because of his hectic work schedule. He continues to repay his car loan as per schedule.

His updated expenses are:

- Rent: Rs 20,000
- Groceries and utilities: Rs 17,000
- Eating out and entertainment: Rs 7000
- Car loan repayment: Rs 15,000

4. Reflecting on financial goals

Rohit's primary financial goal was to accumulate an emergency fund equal to six months' expenses, something he accomplished successfully by the first half of the year. Now, with more income coming his way, he plans on saving towards the down payment on a home while increasing his investments for long-term security.

5. Adjusting the budget

Given Rohit's increased income, lower discretionary spending and new financial goals, he adjusts his budget as follows:

- Rent: Rs 20,000
- Groceries and utilities: Rs 17,000
- Eating out and entertainment: Rs 7000
- Car loan repayment: Rs 15,000

- Savings for house down payment: Rs 25,000
- Investments: Rs 36,000

6. Implementation and tracking

Rohit launches his budget and begins tracking his expenses to stay within it, using an app as his personal finance dashboard for tracking his income, expenses, savings and investments.

Conclusion

Rohit's case illustrates how an annual financial review can lead to a budget that better reflects one's income, spending habits and goals. Now, equipped with his revised budget plan, Rohit can effectively manage his personal finances while working towards his new goals more easily, underscoring the significance of regular budget reviews in successful financial management.

Chapter 13

Portfolio Rebalancing Strategies

Portfolio rebalancing is crucial in managing personal finances and investments. It's the process of adjusting the weightings of the various assets in your portfolio to stay aligned with your original asset allocation strategy. There are two primary types of rebalancing—time-based and threshold or milestone-based.

Time-based rebalancing

Time-based rebalancing involves adjusting your portfolio at regular intervals, either monthly, quarterly, semi-annually or annually, depending on market conditions. This is in order to keep your asset allocation consistent over time, the primary goal being to maintain the consistency of asset allocation across your entire investment strategy portfolio.

- **Establish a timeline:** Establish an annual or more frequent rebalance timeline depending on your investment strategy and availability; making adjustments as required can also help ensure successful rebalancing results.
- **Review your portfolio:** At regular intervals, assess and update the allocations in your current portfolio,

such as in stocks, bonds, real estate and cash. Calculate the percentages that represent these asset classes (i.e., equities, bonds, real estate, cash).

- **Compare with target allocation:** Compare your current allocation with the target allocation, which should reflect your risk tolerance, investment goals and time horizon.
- **Adjust portfolio:** If your current allocation strays significantly from the target allocation, adjust it by selling off assets from overweight categories and buying assets in underweight ones to return your portfolio to its ideal allocation mix. This change should bring it closer to balance again.

Threshold or milestone-based rebalancing

This is done when the proportion of an asset class in your portfolio deviates by a predetermined amount or threshold from the target allocation.

Here is the typical process for threshold-based rebalancing:

- **Set a threshold:** Decide on a specific percentage deviation from your target allocation that would trigger rebalancing. This might be a 5 per cent or 10 per cent deviation, depending on your risk tolerance and investment strategy.
- **Monitor your portfolio:** Regularly review your portfolio's asset allocation. This could be done weekly, monthly, or as needed, based on market conditions and the nature of your investments.
- **Compare with target allocation:** When reviewing, compare the current allocation with your target allocation.

- **Adjust portfolio:** If the allocation to an asset class deviates by more than your set threshold from your target allocation, rebalance your portfolio. This might involve selling off assets in categories that are over the threshold and buying assets in categories that are under the threshold.

Rebalancing helps maintain your portfolio at an appropriate risk level and aligns your investments with your financial goals. Rebalancing may have tax and transaction-cost implications and should be carried out carefully to avoid tax consequences or transaction fees. For this reason, prior to any significant portfolio adjustments for rebalancing, they should always be discussed with an investment professional.

Case study: Sanjana Murthy—Portfolio Rebalancing

Background

Sanjana Murthy, a thirty-five-year-old self-employed graphic designer living in Bengaluru, began investing five years ago. Since then she has created a diverse portfolio featuring 60 per cent equity (such as domestic and international mutual funds), 30 per cent bonds (such as PPF or tax-free bonds) and 10 per cent gold to suit her high risk tolerance, long-term investment horizon and goal of increasing her wealth. Now, after six months have gone by, it's time for a financial review and portfolio rebalancing for Sanjana.

1. Time-based rebalancing

Sanjana has planned for an annual review even at the start of investing. Upon review, her portfolio now comprises 70 per cent equities, 25 per cent bonds and 5 per cent gold investments as a result of strong equity market performance.

Sanjana has an ideal combination of high risk tolerance and long-term goals that allows her to invest more in equity than she has previously. But in order to maintain some balance and remain true to her original strategy, she decides to sell some equity holdings and put the proceeds in bonds and gold investments, thus realigning her portfolio with her target allocation.

2. Threshold or milestone-based rebalancing

Sanjana carefully monitors her portfolio for any deviations from its target allocations, setting an exception threshold of 10 per cent. A few months after the time-based rebalancing, the equity market experiences a sudden uptick, which quickly sees the equity percentage in her portfolio rise to 72 per cent.

Sanjana decides it is time for another rebalancing of the portfolio because her equity holdings have gone past her 10 per cent threshold limit and are now at 11 per cent. To bring them back within her target range, she sells some equity mutual funds and reinvests the proceeds into bonds and gold instruments to achieve her target allocation levels.

Sanjana undertakes regular reviews and adjustments of her investment portfolio, reviewing it every six months to maintain her target allocation, reviewing the asset allocation and making adjustments as necessary.

Conclusion

Sanjana's case illustrates how both time-based and threshold-based portfolio rebalancing strategies can be effectively used in managing an investment portfolio. By regularly reviewing her investments and making the necessary modifications, Sanjana ensures that they continue to meet her financial goals while taking into account market dynamics and her own changing personal circumstances.

Key takeaways from this section

- Review your income, expenses, assets and liabilities regularly
- Review your goals half-yearly
- Review your risk annually
- Review asset allocation annually
- Rebalance your portfolio regularly, based on the reviews

Section 5: Optimize (O)

'Financial success is a journey, a combination of small steps and smart choices that lead to extraordinary results.'
—Unknown

As you progress towards your financial goals, it is important to continually optimize your finances. This involves finding ways to increase your income, reduce your expenses and maximize your savings. Look for ways to save on everyday expenses, such as cutting back on eating out or shopping for bargains. Consider increasing your income through side hustles or additional education or training.

Optimization of a financial plan involves taking steps to ensure that your plan is well-suited to your financial goals and maximizes your savings and potential returns while minimizing the risks. Savings can be increased by increasing one's income and decreasing expenses and liabilities.

Chapter 14

Increasing Income

Increase active income

Attainment of early financial freedom typically involves increasing one's active income—this refers to money earned through work or business, but which requires effort, persistence and continued learning. Assess your skill set, market demand and personal interests in order to identify strategies for maximizing your earning potential while prioritizing work-life balance and self-care practices so as to avoid burnout while striving for financial freedom.

Here are a few strategies that will help you increase your active income:

1. Invest in your education

Investment in education can be an excellent way to expand your income potential and open doors to new opportunities. By expanding and improving your knowledge base, education helps you develop your abilities further and expands the skill set you already possess. Staying abreast of industry trends, technologies and best practices is essential if you wish to position yourself as an attractive job candidate or business entrepreneur in today's job market. Upskilling or seeking advanced degrees and certifications can make you more attractive as an applicant for higher-paying roles or allow you to provide services that command higher rates, as well as provide you with greater insight and critical-thinking abilities. Education also broadens your perspective. Education provides you with opportunities to develop your problem-solving, creative thinking and analytical abilities, which are highly valued in today's job market and will open the doors to higher-level roles with added responsibilities and income potential. Remember, education is an investment worth making, and it can change your trajectory of earnings throughout your lifetime!

2. Advance your career

Take steps to advance in your career by prioritizing professional development and taking steps towards professional advancement. This could involve learning new skills, enrolling for higher education or certification programmes, networking effectively with colleagues and seeking promotions or salary increases during performance reviews. Make a case that justifies higher compensation for you through industry benchmark research when you negotiate for a higher salary during performance reviews. Research the industry norms in your sector to support your case!

3. Launch side hustles

Consider starting a side business or taking on freelance projects to generate additional income. Leverage your skills, hobbies or passions to offer services or products people are willing to pay for, or leverage any specialized knowledge you may possess by offering consulting services, coaching services or online training as a way of sharing what you know while earning revenue in return.

4. Establish your brand online

Utilize platforms such as LinkedIn or create a professional website, building an impressive personal brand online that showcases your skills, experience and achievements to attract higher-paying job offers or freelance opportunities.

5. Leverage your network

A network of people from various backgrounds and skill levels can come together for mutual gain. Tapping into one can open doors to opportunities like job referrals, business collaborations and mentorship as well as find you income-generation prospects not otherwise easily available through traditional channels.

6. Invest in yourself

Investing in yourself will enable you to stay abreast of industry trends and technological innovations, make use of opportunities for continuous learning and remain relevant in today's changing marketplace. Adaptability allows businesses to remain relevant while seizing on opportunities as they emerge. Investment in your health and well-being can have an equally dramatic effect on your income potential. By prioritizing physical exercise as well as mental rejuvenation, you can increase your productivity, energy levels, performance and earnings potential, leading to higher earning power overall. Lastly, investing in yourself shows your commitment to both personal and professional growth, which may open doors to more opportunities, collaborations and mentorships. Networking and building relationships with like-minded individuals could open the doors to higher-paying positions, business partnerships or entrepreneurial endeavours.

7. Launch your own business

Starting a business can be the key to increasing your income and achieving financial success. Aside from giving you unlimited earning potential, your own business can be in alignment with your passions and provide you with financial freedom. Although starting your own business involves risks and difficulties, with proper planning, execution and perseverance, it can become a rewarding and lucrative endeavour. Simply identify market needs or niches in existing ventures for which there exists potential for growth and profit-making and launch your business.

Increase passive income

Passive income refers to income generated with minimal effort or time commitment on your part as you pursue your main activity. Establishing multiple passive sources of income will provide you stability and increase the chances of early financial freedom for you.

Here are a few strategies for expanding your passive income:

1. Rental properties or REITs

Rental properties can offer you a steady stream of rental income, potential tax benefits and long-term appreciation potential. Residential or commercial properties that boast of these features should be carefully considered for investment to achieve steady cash flows as well as long-term appreciation potential. Real estate investment trusts (REITs), on the other hand, allow investors to gain exposure to market performance through dividend payments.

2. Renting out assets

Rental assets can bring easy and passive income, and you can realize the full value of your possessions. Renting out spare rooms in your home, vacant properties, vehicles or equipment is one great way of creating passive income and realizing your assets' true potential value. OYO rooms, Airbnb, Zoomcar—platforms make connecting with potential renters simpler than ever before. By setting competitive rental rates through these platforms, passive income can be earned without actively having to work towards it. Just ensure your assets remain well maintained, adequately insured and meet the local regulations; effective management and marketing can unlock an ongoing source of passive income for you!

3. Invest in mutual funds and exchange-traded funds (ETFs)

Mutual funds and ETFs are other excellent investment vehicles from which to earn passive income, providing you with access to professional fund managers, diversification benefits and potential long-term capital appreciation potential, as well as regular dividend payouts adding to the passive income stream! It is crucial to select funds that match your goals, risk tolerance and time horizon, as this ensures the continued generation of passive income from the investments in your portfolio. Rebalancing of your assets can ensure maximum returns from them and ongoing generation of passive income from your investments over time. Regular monitoring/rebalancing will optimize returns while guaranteeing ongoing passive income generation.

4. Dividend-paying stocks

Consider investing in stocks that offer consistent dividend payments; additionally, consider reinvesting the dividend income to accelerate investment growth.

5. Peer-to-peer (P2P) lending platforms

Peer-to-peer lending platforms act as intermediaries between those seeking funds and individual investors looking for returns from lending money through these platforms and earning interest on the loans. P2P lending presents an excellent way to diversify your investment portfolio and potentially earn greater returns than from conventional fixed-income instruments. However, to minimize the risks involved, it's crucial that due diligence be conducted on prospective borrowers by doing in-depth background checks on them and assessing their creditworthiness. You will also need to diversify your loans across multiple borrowers to reduce your risk. India's P2P lending platforms are regulated by the Reserve Bank of India for investor protection and transparency. By using them you can gain passive income while actively contributing towards expanding India's lending market.

6. Fixed deposits/Provident Fund/Public Provident Fund

Indian investors seeking stable returns often turn to fixed-income instruments like fixed deposits (FD), Provident Fund (PF) and Public Provident Fund (PPF) for income generation. These instruments offer a predetermined interest rate and ensure a steady income stream over an agreed-upon period. FDs provide flexibility with tenure and payout options, while PPF and PF schemes serve as long-term retirement savings plans with tax benefits. By investing in these instruments, individuals can generate regular interest income while protecting their capital. When analysing returns from these investments, it's essential to factor in inflation rates, tax implications and compound interest. Creating a balanced portfolio with both fixed-income assets and growth-oriented assets can help mitigate the risks while optimizing income generation.

7. Sovereign gold bonds

Sovereign gold bonds (SGBs), introduced by the Reserve Bank of India (RBI), provide individuals with a convenient and safe means of investing in gold without physical ownership of it or the associated risks. They provide investors an opportunity to participate in the potential price appreciation of this precious metal without needing physical ownership of it. Each bond is denominated in grams of gold, and the government-issued instrument carries an interest rate of 2.5 per cent annually, which is determined by government decree, with an eight-year maturity date.

8. Develop and market digital products

One approach to making passive income is through developing and marketing digital products, especially given the rapid expansion of the digital economy. Individuals can leverage their skills and expertise in order to design and market a variety of digital offerings, utilizing various strategies that are available today. Digital products encompass everything from books and online courses to software applications, templates, stock photos, music downloads, stock photography services and music tracks. By creating digital products you can tap into an expansive online market while reaching multiple target markets and make money around the clock. Identification of market needs and preferences, provision of valuable content, leveraging of local online platforms, social media channels and targeted marketing strategies are crucial aspects to successfully selling digital products online. By capitalizing on the technology-powered landscape of today and harnessing its power for the sale of digital goods, you can earn passive income.

9. Affiliate marketing

Affiliate marketing can be an excellent way to generate passive income online by advertising products or services on a network such as the Internet. By joining affiliate programmes and becoming associated with companies through them, affiliate marketers can partner up and earn commissions when referrals or sales happen through their unique affiliate link. Affiliate marketing provides the unique advantage of creating income without needing to deal with product creation, inventory management and customer support directly. Once your affiliate marketing campaigns and content creation efforts are in place and potential customers start making purchases via your affiliate links, passive income can come pouring in. In order to maximize your passive income potential, it's key to select relevant and high-quality products while building an engaged audience base as well as optimizing your marketing efforts.

10. Royalties from intellectual property

Royalty payments on intellectual property can provide creators with a source of passive income from their original creations. Patents, copyrights, trademarks and trade secrets fall in this category of income-generating properties. By licensing or selling their intellectual property rights, creators can earn ongoing royalties. Authors receive royalties from book sales; musicians from music streaming or sales; and inventors through the licensing of their patented inventions. Royalties provide an effective passive source of revenue. To maximize revenue potential and secure revenues effectively through this kind of property, it's critical that intellectual property rights are properly managed using contracts, licensing agreements and enforcement mechanisms put in place to maximize your revenues and earnings potential.

11. Create a YouTube channel or podcast

Starting a YouTube channel or podcast can be an effective way of increasing your revenue streams. You can earn revenue from advertisements, sponsored content sales, affiliate marketing commissions, merchandise sales and crowdfunding. With digital media's growing influence and the increasing popularity of online content platforms, you can reach wider audiences with your message and make money from it. However, ensuring success here requires consistent effort, quality creations that engage the target audiences well and proper promotion strategies.

Chapter 15

Reduce Expenses and Liabilities

Reduce discretionary expenses

Reducing your discretionary expenses is essential for managing your personal finances and reaching your financial goals. By controlling your non-essential spending and minimizing non-essential purchases, you can save money, lower your debt load and build a stronger financial foundation. Here are a few strategies for effectively decreasing your discretionary expenditure.

Establishing a budget is vitally important. Start by tracking all your expenses over one month to see exactly where your money is being spent. Categorize the expenses under needs, desires and dreams and identify areas where they can be reduced. With an adequate plan in place, you will gain greater insight into your current financial state as well as make more informed choices regarding your discretionary spending decisions.

Prioritizing needs over desires is key to effective decision-making. When faced with the temptation to purchase impulse items, ask yourself if it truly meets an immediate or future necessity or could possibly wait. By differentiating between needs and desires, you can reduce unnecessary expenses and channel funds towards more meaningful goals.

Dining-out bills can quickly add up. Instead, why not cook and pack meals yourself to save money and take care of your health? By planning for and buying groceries in bulk and prepping in advance for your meals, you can further cut expenses and avoid frequent eating out.

Entertainment expenses can eat into discretionary spending significantly. Find low-cost or free alternatives for leisure activities, such as attending community events or visiting parks instead of movie theatres, reading, exercising or practising music. It may be possible to significantly cut your entertainment expenditure without cutting down on your enjoyment of art or entertainment! By reviewing how you spend your leisure time, you can significantly decrease your expenses without giving up enjoyable activities!

Subscriptions and memberships should also be considered. Assess their worth to you, cancelling those that are no longer necessary (think streaming services, gym memberships, magazine subscriptions). Look for free or less costly alternatives; they might bring you similar results.

Transportation expenses can quickly add up when using your private car as a single passenger, so look for more cost-efficient means of transportation, such as public transport, carpooling or biking whenever possible. Not only will this lower your fuel bills but it will also contribute towards your leading a greener lifestyle!

As you shop, take an approach designed to save you money. Compare prices on different platforms and look out for sales/discounts. Consider generic or store brands instead of premium ones; plan ahead for your shopping trips and create and stick to an accurate shopping list. This will save you from unnecessarily spending on items that do not immediately serve your needs.

Energy usage can also provide savings opportunities. Select energy-saving appliances and devices that consume less power. Turn off lights, unplug electronic devices when they are not necessary and utilize natural lighting whenever possible for maximum savings on electricity bills. Small changes such as these can add up quickly.

Travel expenses can be a big drain on finances. While travelling is often desirable, it's wise to plan and budget carefully when making plans and booking accommodations. Search for affordable lodging options, use price-comparison websites when possible and consider travelling during off-peak seasons when prices may be cheaper. Prioritize destinations that offer good value-for-money experiences and explore local attractions that fit your budget.

As it can be challenging to pursue expensive hobbies or activities, finding inexpensive recreational alternatives such as walking, cycling, hiking or visiting public parks is essential in terms of keeping your discretionary spending in check while enjoying leisure activities. Engage in low-cost or free recreational options, like those mentioned earlier. You can also attend local cultural events that will not break your wallet. By exploring less costly hobbies and leisure activities, you can still enjoy your free time while keeping your discretionary spending under control.

Overall, cutting discretionary expenses requires conscious decision-making and commitment to financial discipline. Establishing a budget, differentiating between needs and desires and adopting frugal habits are vital steps in decreasing your discretionary expenses and meeting your financial goals more quickly. By consistently monitoring your spending patterns through the implementation of these strategies, you will drastically reduce your discretionary expenditure, saving more money and moving faster in the direction of financial stability.

Review financial statements to reduce leakages

Case study: Parag Patel—Analysing Financial Statements and Minimizing Discretionary Expenses

Background

Parag Patel, an Indian working professional, is concerned about his financial status and wants to review his financial statements so as to identify the areas where he can reduce his discretionary expenses to achieve his long-term savings goals. With this in mind, Parag undertakes an in-depth audit and implements the necessary modifications.

Step 1: Gathering financial statements

Parag initiates this process by gathering his bank, credit card and utility statements as well as noting down any recurring expenses like rent payments, insurance premiums or loan repayments to gain an in-depth view of his present obligations. This step gives him clarity as to the current state of his finances.

Step 2: Examining income and expenses

Next, Parag carefully considers his income and expenses. First, he evaluates his monthly pay from both his job and his extra sources of income. Next, he divides up the expenses between fixed (such as rent, utility bills, loan EMIs and insurance premiums) and discretionary (entertainment/dining out/shopping subscriptions/travel).

Step 3: Identification of discretionary expenses

Parag performs a careful audit of his discretionary expenses to identify areas where he can save. He has further divided them into essential and non-essential categories—the essential spends bring genuine joy or value while the non-essential spends can either be reduced or done away with altogether.

Step 4: Establishment of priorities and goals

Parag develops his financial priorities and long-term goals. This step allows him to synchronize his spending habits with his objectives of saving, investing and reducing his debts. With clear goals before him, Parag becomes even more motivated to reduce unnecessary expenditure and direct the money thus saved towards meeting these priorities.

Step 5: Implementation of strategies to decrease discretionary expenses

To reduce his discretionary expenses, Parag implements several strategies. These include:

a) Meal planning and cooking at home

Parag starts planning his meals in advance and cooking at home to reduce his dining-out expenses. He embraces cost-effective cooking methods and explores new recipes, and his meals have become more enjoyable though he has significantly cut down on food costs.

b) Audit of subscriptions

Parag assesses his subscription services, cancelling those that no longer bring him significant value or which he can do without. These include streaming platforms, magazine subscriptions and other recurring expenditures that provide little tangible gains for him.

c) Entertainment alternatives

Parag actively explores low-cost or free entertainment alternatives. These include visits to the local parks, libraries and cultural events where he can engage in leisurely pursuits without incurring large expenses.

d) Smart shopping

Parag is an informed shopper and is adept at carefully comparing prices, using coupons, taking advantage of sales promotions and discounts and creating and sticking to shopping lists to avoid impulse buys or any unnecessary expenses.

e) Energy conservation

To bring down his utility bills, Parag adopts energy-conserving practices such as turning off the lights and electronic gadgets when they are not in use, purchasing energy-saving appliances and optimizing the use of air conditioning.

f) Travel planning

Parag carefully plans each trip he makes, searching for budget accommodation, booking flights during off-peak seasons to save on travel costs and prioritizing budget-friendly destinations. By being strategic with his expenses, he achieves significant savings.

Step 6: Regular monitoring and adjustments

Parag understands the significance of monitoring expenses closely and making the necessary adjustments regularly. To this end, he conducts regular reviews of his financial statements to compare actual expenditure with the budgeted amounts. This enables him to quickly detect areas where overspending has taken place and take corrective actions as quickly as possible.

Results

Parag sees remarkable changes in his financial situation after his careful review and implementation of strategies to cut his discretionary expenses. His savings rise significantly and he is able to allocate additional funds towards investments and debt repayment. He is now moving closer towards his long-term financial goals. He has also developed mindful spending habits that will benefit him over time.

Loan management

Individuals looking to increase their savings and achieve their financial goals more rapidly should prioritize and pay off their loans strategically, in an orderly fashion. Here is a step-by-step guide on effectively ranking loans for repayment:

Step 1: Analyse your loan portfolio

Begin by gathering details of all of your loans—your outstanding balances, the interest rates and monthly payment amounts against any personal, credit card, student, car or other loans you might have taken.

Step 2: Understand what interest rates you are paying

Inspect each loan's interest rate. Loans with higher interest rates usually cost you more in the long run; thus it is wise to prioritize paying them off first.

Step 3: Establish loan repayment priorities

To assign priority for repayment purposes, rank all your loans according to their interest rates, starting with those featuring the highest rates as your priority loan(s). These loans should receive top priority when it comes to repayment.

Step 4: Make the minimum payments

To avoid penalties or negative impacts on your credit history, always pay at least the minimum monthly payments on all loans to protect both yourself and your credit score.

Step 5: Allocate extra funds for repayment of loans

If you have extra money available, use it to pay off loans of higher interest rates while continuing to make the minimum payments on others. This strategy helps you save on interest costs in the long run.

Step 6: Snowball or avalanche method of paying off loans

There are two popular approaches for paying off loans: the snowball method and the avalanche method.

The snowball method

Under this strategy, the focus should be on repayment of loans with smaller balances first while making the minimum payments on others. When that loan has been eliminated, continue this approach with the next smallest loan and the next and so on, until all have been resolved. Gradually build momentum as each debt disappears. This approach provides psychological relief as you see your loans cleared away and gives you the motivation to continue on your debt repayment journey.

The avalanche method

In this strategy, the aim is to pay off loans with higher interest rates first while making minimum payments on other loans. By prioritizing high-interest debts first and making smaller monthly payments on other debts, you could potentially reduce your overall interest payments over time and save even more than from traditional approaches to clearing loans, such as snowballing.

Step 7: Monitoring and making adjustments

You should regularly review your loan repayment progress and adjust your finances as loans get paid off. As each one goes away, reallocate the funds you had earlier set aside for it towards repayment of other debts, thus speeding up debt consolidation.

Step 8: Recognize your achievements

Remember and celebrate each step along your journey as you pay back loans with discipline and perseverance. Acknowledgement of milestones can keep your motivation up over the course of repayment!

Step 9: Contemplate refinancing or consolidation

If you have multiple loans with high interest rates, consolidating them into one lower-interest loan could help simplify repayment and potentially cut costs by streamlining and bringing down interest costs.

Step 10: Focus on savings

As you pay off your loans, use some of the money originally allocated for debt payment towards savings. An emergency fund and your long-term goals should become your top priorities once your high-interest debts have been cleared.

Maintain a realistic outlook. Repayment is a gradual process that demands discipline, perseverance and an effective financial plan. By prioritizing loans for repayment and sticking to your goals you will significantly increase your savings and achieve financial independence more rapidly than you would have otherwise.

Chapter 16

Minimize Taxes, Fees and Risk

Minimize taxes

Minimizing taxes is an integral component of financial optimization in India. By understanding the tax laws and devising effective strategies to deal with your investments from the perspective of tax, you can legally reduce your tax liabilities and keep more of your earnings for yourself. Here we explore various methods and provisions available in India for minimizing your taxes.

1. Take advantage of tax deductions and exemptions

One key way to lower tax liability in India is to take advantage of the tax deductions and exemptions granted under the Income-tax Act. Deductions are expenses or investments allowed to be subtracted from the total taxable income. Deductions reduce one's tax liability. Tax deductions and exemptions apply for contributions made to various funds or policies such as the Public Provident Fund (PPF), Employee Provident Fund (EPF), National Pension System (NPS), life insurance premiums, tuition fees for children's education and repayment of home loans. Tax deductions also apply to contributions made towards health insurance for your family or your parents and towards critical illness.

2. Opt for tax-saving investments

Investments in tax-saving instruments not only help individuals save for their future but also provide them with tax benefits. The government encourages such investments by offering deductions against them under Section 80C of the Income-tax Act. Some popular tax-saving instruments include:

- *Equity-linked savings scheme (ELSS):* The ELSS is a type of mutual fund that offers tax benefits and potential long-term capital appreciation.
- *Public Provident Fund (PPF):* This is a government-backed savings scheme that offers tax-free interest income and a deduction on contributions.
- *National Savings Certificate (NSC):* This is a fixed-income investment instrument that offers tax benefits and guaranteed returns.
- *Tax-saving fixed deposits:* Banks offer fixed deposit schemes, with a lock-in period of five years, that provide tax benefits.
- *Sukanya Samriddhi Yojana (SSY):* This is a government-backed savings scheme, for your daughter, that offers tax-free interest income and a deduction on contributions.

3. Maximize your contribution to retirement funds

Contributions to retirement funds like the Employee Provident Fund (EPF) and National Pension System (NPS) bring both tax advantages and long-term financial security for employees. Employee contributions made under Section 80C qualify for tax deduction, while employer contributions are tax-free. Similarly, contributions to NPS qualify for deduction under both Sections 80CCD(1) and (2) as they accrue tax savings benefits over time.

4. Plan your capital gains

Capital gains generated from selling assets such as real estate or stocks in India are taxed. However, certain provisions that can reduce the tax liabilities associated with them exist. Long-term gains (assets held for more than twenty-four months) on listed equities and equity-oriented mutual funds can qualify for exemption under specific guidelines, and individuals investing within certain time frames in specified bonds (CGAS or similar schemes) or residential property could potentially qualify for further exemption.

5. Look for tax-efficient salary components

Revamp your salary components and structure them in a tax-efficient way to minimize taxes. Employees can negotiate to allocate more of their salary towards allowances eligible for tax exemption, like house rent allowance (HRA), leave travel allowance (LTA) or medical benefits that qualify. Likewise, opting for flexible salary components, like meal coupons, can offer tax advantages too.

6. Plan investments for dividend income

Dividend income is tax-liable in the hands of the recipient, so in order to minimize taxes on this form of income, individuals can plan their investments so as to obtain dividends from tax-efficient sources. For instance, dividends received through ownership of equity shares and equity-oriented mutual funds may be tax-exempt up to certain limits. So, investing in these instruments could maximize your tax-free dividend income.

7. Keep to the tax deadlines

Staying organized and compliant with tax filing and payment deadlines is critical in avoiding penalties and interest charges, including for late filing of income tax returns and advance tax payments as well as submission of the required tax forms or documents.

8. Get professional advice

Navigating India's complex tax laws can be a difficult exercise. For best results in tax planning and optimization, seek guidance and insight from tax professionals or chartered accountants, who will tell you what specific deductions, exemptions and investments will suit your financial status and goals.

9. Keep up with the tax laws in India

Indian tax regulations can change quickly. In order to stay aware of all the available opportunities for saving taxes and reducing expenses, you need to regularly look up the updated legislation as well as seek professional advice on any alterations introduced by the government. This can keep you fully aware of the new tax amendments, exemptions and deductions available in India.

10. Maintain the necessary documents

Proper documentation is an integral component of tax planning and compliance. Individuals must keep records of their income, expenses, investments and supporting documents like receipts, invoices or investment statements, which could prove invaluable when it comes to assessments or audit of their taxes.

Conclusion

Tax minimization is an integral component of financial planning in India. By taking advantage of the available deductions, exemptions, tax-saving investments and strategies, you can optimize your finances while decreasing your tax liabilities. Therefore, it's vital that you remain informed about the latest developments on the tax front, seek professional advice when necessary and maintain adequate documentation in order to effectively optimize your taxes.

Case study: Surya Chadda—Tax Minimization Strategy

Background

Surya Chadda is working as a doctor with an annual salary of Rs 15 lakh. He committed to minimizing his tax bill and saving as much money as possible from taxes. For this goal, he seeks professional guidance and executes an in-depth strategy aimed at tax minimization. Here's more of what it involves:

Scenario 1: Income tax without tax minimization

Surya does not invest in any tax-saving instruments. He is thus eligible only for a standard deduction of Rs 50,000. Surya's taxable income will be Rs 14,50,000 on which the income tax, including cess and surcharge, will be approximately Rs 2,57,400.

Scenario 2: Income tax with tax minimization

Surya invests Rs 60,000 in PPF and Rs 70,000 in a five-year tax-saving fixed deposit with a post office (PO). He also buys a term insurance policy for which he pays a premium of Rs 20,000. Surya also buys a family floater health insurance policy for which the annual premium is Rs 25,000. Additionally, he invests in a residential home on which the interest component is Rs 1,00,000.

Surya thus claims a Rs 1,50,000 deduction under Section 80C of the Income-tax Act, Rs 25,000 under Section 80D and finally Rs 1,00,000 under Section 80EE. With these deductions, his taxable income will be Rs 12,25,000 on which the income tax will be approximately Rs 1,87,200. Surya's investments in tax minimization instruments have thus saved him Rs 70,200.

Scenario 3: Income Tax compensation re-structuring

Surya negotiates with the hospital to appoint him as a consulting professional instead of a salaried employee. He opts for the presumptive scheme of income tax under Section 44ADA wherein he can claim only 50 per cent of his gross earnings as taxable income. Surya's taxable income will be Rs 7,50,000 on which the income tax, including cess and surcharge, will be approximately Rs 65,000. He thus saves Rs 1,92,400 as compared to Scenario 1, which can be invested towards his financial goals.

Surya implements a thorough tax minimization strategy, which helps him significantly lower his tax liabilities while optimizing his savings and investments. By aligning his financial goals with his tax planning strategies, Surya achieves greater efficiency of use for his income and resources.

Minimize premium for insurance

Reducing insurance premiums for health and life policies

Insurance is an integral component of financial planning, offering protection and peace of mind in the matter of unpredictable situations. But the premiums you have to pay may strain your budget. There are various strategies you can utilize to lower the health and life insurance premiums you have to pay by being proactive in making informed choices. You'll strike a good balance between coverage and affordability by being proactive about it all! Here are a few effective techniques:

1. Assess your coverage needs

Begin by determining your coverage needs. Assess both your health and life insurance needs, going by factors like your age, health condition, lifestyle needs and financial situation in order to accurately gauge their significance for you. Doing this allows you to avoid over-insuring and paying unnecessary premiums.

2. Live a healthy lifestyle

Insurance companies often factor in your health condition and lifestyle factors when setting premiums. Adopting healthy behaviours, including maintaining a balanced diet, regularly exercising, giving up tobacco use and avoiding excessive alcohol consumption, etc., could qualify you for lower premiums from some providers. Furthermore, there are wellness programmes within many insurance policies that reward policyholders who pursue a healthy lifestyle.

3. Compare insurance plans

Don't settle for the first plan you find when searching for health and life insurance policies. Make the effort and time to compare health and life plans from multiple insurers for comprehensive coverage at cost-effective premiums—online insurance aggregators can be invaluable resources here!

4. Opt for higher deductibles

Deductibles represent the out-of-pocket expenses you must cover before insurance coverage kicks in. Your choosing higher deductibles could decrease the premium amounts. However, make sure they remain an affordable amount should any claims arise.

5. Choose family floater plans

If you have children, family floater plans that cover multiple family members under one policy could offer significant cost advantages. Be sure that the coverage limits and benefits suit every member of the household adequately.

6. Review and update your coverage regularly

As your circumstances shift with marriage, parenthood or increases in income, make sure your insurance policies match up accordingly, perhaps by increasing some kinds of coverage while decreasing others, to ensure that you pay only for what is necessary without incurring an unnecessary premium burden.

7. Secure no-claim bonuses

Many health insurance policies feature no-claim bonuses as an incentive for customers to live a healthy lifestyle and reduce claims over time. This leads to reduced premiums as no-claim bonuses accumulate over time and reduce the premium costs.

8. Purchase insurance early

Insurance premium rates tend to be significantly lower when purchased at a younger age; insurers perceive younger individuals as facing fewer health risks than older individuals and offer them discounted premium rates. So it would be prudent to start your coverage as early as possible for maximum cost-savings potential.

9. Opt for term insurance as life coverage

Term insurance provides cost-effective life coverage compared with other forms of life coverage policies, providing a high sum assured for lower premium costs overall and without investment components. So this choice is cost-effective and attractive to people primarily concerned about protecting themselves financially during unexpected events.

10. Seek professional advice

Seeking expert guidance is often beneficial when it comes to insurance. Consider consulting an independent adviser or financial planner who can assess your needs and guide you through all available coverage, providing personalized recommendations aligned with your financial goals.

Strive for an equilibrium between affordability and protection levels that meet your requirements.

Minimize fees

Minimizing fees is key to increasing savings in India as it affects the overall returns you get from your investments. It can be another way to maximize your savings and potentially achieve your financial goals faster. Let's examine some strategies for decreasing fees and expanding savings here in India.

1. Select low-cost investment options

One effective strategy for minimizing fees is to select lower-cost investment vehicles such as mutual funds and ETFs that charge lower expense ratios than others. These funds generally charge lower fees and offer a greater return potential overall. By opting for cheaper investments, you're more likely to retain more of your returns and boost savings over time.

2. Choose direct plans of mutual funds

When investing in mutual funds, select direct plans rather than the regular ones to reduce the fees and commissions associated with distributors or agents. Direct plans also feature lower expense ratios than their regular counterparts. So you save both in terms of fees and investment money.

3. Avoid load funds

Some mutual funds charge exit loads when their units are sold. This leads to additional fees upon their sale. To minimize fees and maximize your savings potential, opt for mutual funds with either no or lower exit charges.

4. Consider discount brokers for stock trading

When engaging in stock trading, discount brokers offer lower brokerage fees. This leads to reduced transaction costs for the customer. Look for brokers offering competitive rates and reliable trading platforms as they will enable you to save more as the brokerage costs will be less. You will save money on every trade and increase your overall savings.

5. Use technology and online platforms

Utilize technology and online investment platforms to reduce costs. Financial institutions and fintech companies often offer affordable investment products through these channels, charging lower fees than the traditional channels. Plus, this approach often gives you access to an assortment of investment products and tools at lower costs, so you increase your savings over time.

6. Contemplate passive investment strategies

Passive investment options such as index funds and ETFs offer investors reduced-cost alternatives by replicating the market-index performance without active management costs being involved. Usually, these passive funds have lower expense ratios than actively managed funds, making them suitable choices for long-term investors looking for lower expenses.

7. Regularly review and rebalance your portfolio

Regularly review and rebalance your investment portfolio to make sure it matches your financial goals. Adjust the allocations when necessary to maintain your risk profile, avoid transactions that call for additional fees, and maximize returns and savings by keeping your portfolio in alignment with your goals. By doing this you'll maximize returns while saving more!

8. Be aware of account fees

Compare the account fees associated with various financial products such as savings accounts, trading accounts and demat accounts from different institutions to identify those that offer low or no account fees and allow you to save more and reduce unnecessary expenses.

9. Seek professional advice

A financial planner or adviser can be invaluable for guiding you through the investment landscape and pinpointing cost-cutting strategies. This person will meet with you to assess your investment goals, risk tolerance and needs and help you make informed decisions that enable you to minimize fees and increase savings.

10. Educate yourself

Make the effort to become informed on investment options, fees and their effects on savings. Keep yourself up to date with industry trends, regulatory changes and any new investment products. By staying knowledgeable, you'll make more informed choices while simultaneously becoming more likely to negotiate better agreements or reduce fees and charges effectively.

By following these strategies, individuals in India can minimize fees and expenses related to investments, ultimately increasing their savings.

Case study: Impact of Fees on Investing

Let's use an illustration to demonstrate the impact fees can have on long-term savings. Imagine you want to invest in a mutual fund that has an average annual return of 15 per cent over thirty years. Your two options for investment are A, with an expense ratio of 0.5 per cent, and B, with 1.5 per cent.

Option A: You would have invested Rs 3.60 crore after thirty years (Rs 10,000 multiplied by twelve months and thirty years). The value of your investment with an earning of 15 per cent annual returns and fees of 0.5 per cent will be about Rs 4.75 crore.

Option B: Here again you would have invested Rs 3.60 crore after thirty years (Rs 10,000 multiplied by twelve months and thirty years). The value of your investment with an earning of 15 per cent annual returns and fees of 1.5 per cent will be about Rs 3.88 crore. The absolute return drops by approximately 18 per cent.

Fee differences might seem minor at first glance. However, their long-term impact can be significant. By choosing

Option A over Option B over thirty years you would accumulate approximately Rs 87 lakh more savings owing to the lower fees associated with Option A.

This illustration vividly shows how fees can impede savings over time. Even seemingly minor differences in fees can lead to substantial changes in the final investment values. By selecting investments with reduced fees, you're more likely to retain more of your returns, allowing your savings to grow faster over time.

Managing risk

Managing risk and optimizing risk-adjusted returns are integral to effective financial management. They involve identifying the potential threats, developing risk reduction plans and making informed investment decisions that balance risk with reward. By understanding the relationship between risk and returns, individuals and investors alike can maximize financial outcomes while protecting their assets.

One of the first steps in managing risk involves recognizing and assessing the various forms of risks that you can encounter. They could be market, credit, liquidity or geopolitical risks. Each form of risk has its unique qualities and potential ramifications on investment portfolios and financial goals. It is vital to conduct thorough risk analyses in order to identify and get a full picture of the key threats to your financial security.

Once the risks are identified and properly understood, the next step would be to implement mitigation strategies to lessen their impact on your investment portfolio. Diversification is a popular risk mitigation technique, involving the spreading of your investments among different asset classes, sectors and geographic regions in order to dilute the concentration risk among various investments and reduce it significantly. Asset allocation, where investments are made in different assets according to your risk tolerance or objectives, also serves to manage risks effectively.

Risk management also means setting realistic expectations regarding your potential returns. Investors need to recognize that higher returns come with increased levels of risk. As one famous phrase states: *'Return of capital is more important than return on capital.'* Risk-return trade-off is a foundational principle in finance, which says that in order to secure higher returns, investors must accept higher risks. Finding an acceptable compromise that fits both an investor's risk tolerance and goals is the goal, so you need to assess your risk appetite and decide on an acceptable level of risk before making informed decisions about what risks you will take to achieve your desired returns.

Risk-adjusted returns take into account both the risk taken and the returns achieved to provide investors with an accurate picture. Simply looking at returns without considering the associated risks cannot suffice; risk-adjusted returns help investors evaluate the efficiency of their investments as well as compare different investment opportunities.

When analysing risk-adjusted returns, it's critical to keep in mind the risk-free rate, typically represented by government bonds (e.g. ten-year G-sec yield in India). The risk-free rate serves as an objective benchmark against which to measure investments; their returns must exceed this benchmark rate so as to justify the additional risks taken.

Common risk-adjusted performance measures include the Sharpe ratio and the Sortino ratio. These are two widely recognized risk-adjusted performance measures that assess the excess return earned per unit of risk to gauge returns relative to the downside risks. By studying risk-adjusted returns, individuals can assess the success of their investment strategies and adjust them as necessary.

Risk management requires keeping abreast of market conditions and regularly reviewing investment portfolios—

both being dynamic, they fluctuate rapidly with changing circumstances, making it essential to adapt your investments and maintain a well-diversified and risk-managed portfolio. Regular portfolio reviews allow individuals to detect any risks or imbalances and make the necessary changes, keeping risks personally manageable. Keeping abreast of economic indicators, market trends and geopolitical events can assist individuals in anticipating and mitigating risks more effectively.

Risk management must also include a contingency plan in case of unexpected events, which might involve creating an emergency fund to cover unexpected expenses or buying insurance to protect against significant financial losses. Establishing such a safeguard gives individuals peace of mind while lessening the potential impact of unexpected happenings on their financial well-being.

Engaging professional advice when necessary is also of critical importance. Financial advisers and investment professionals provide invaluable expertise when it comes to mitigating risk and optimizing risk-adjusted returns. They help individuals develop comprehensive financial plans, assess their risk tolerance levels and make investment decisions in line with their goals and desired risk-adjusted returns. Professional guidance provides individuals with both the confidence and knowledge necessary for successfully navigating complex markets while optimizing their risk-adjusted returns.

At its core, risk management and achievement of risk-adjusted returns are central elements of effective financial management. By identifying risks, implementing risk-mitigation strategies, making informed investment decisions, diversifying and adopting asset allocation strategies, setting realistic expectations, analysing the risk-adjusted returns over time, staying informed about current developments in their area of investment, as well as by seeking professional advice, individuals can enhance their investment outcomes while protecting their assets against an ever-evolving landscape of risk.

Case study: Sukhdev Singh—Managing Risk

Background

Sukhdev Singh, a thirty-five-year-old Indian investor with an impressive investment portfolio, understands the necessity of managing risk to safeguard his investments and achieve his long-term financial goals. We will examine his approach to risk management where he has utilized various risk reduction strategies while diversifying his investment portfolio.

1. Asset allocation

Sukhdev starts by creating an asset allocation mix that ensures an optimized investment portfolio with balanced exposure to different asset classes such as stocks, bonds, real estate and commodities. Diversifying his investments across these various classes helps him minimize any one specific risk while mitigating the effect of market fluctuations on his overall holdings.

2. Risk evaluation

Sukhdev conducts a detailed risk evaluation of each of his investments, carefully considering factors like market, credit and liquidity risks. By understanding his investments' associated risks, he can make informed decisions to optimize and diversify his portfolio accordingly.

3. Research and due diligence

Sukhdev carefully conducts extensive research before making his investment decisions, conducting in-depth analyses of company finances, economic trends and the performance of the various sectors he's investing in. This allows him to make more informed choices while decreasing the risks related to investing in underperforming or financially unstable entities.

4. Portfolio review

Sukhdev conducts regular reviews of his investment portfolio to make sure it satisfies both his risk tolerance and financial goals, monitoring the market trends and performance of individual investments and then adapting them as required. By remaining vigilant and proactive, Sukhdev can identify any emerging risks promptly and mitigate them quickly.

5. Risk-management tools

For effective risk management, Sukhdev uses various risk-management tools like stop-loss orders and trailing stop orders to limit potential losses by automatically selling securities when their price dips below an agreed-upon level. By employing such strategies, he can protect his investments against sudden market downturns while mitigating any large financial risks that might otherwise be incurred.

6. Emergency fund

Sukhdev understands the significance of setting aside an emergency fund from his income in a liquid savings account for unexpected expenses or emergencies that may arise. Such a fund offers him financial protection by helping him reduce the risks related to investments, such as selling prematurely when times become uncertain.

7. Diversifying across sectors and geographies

Sukhdev also diversifies his investments across different industries and geographies in order to minimize sector or region-specific risks to his portfolio and improve the overall stability of his investments. Diversification helps spread risk while also protecting him against unexpected outcomes arising from his investments.

8. Risk education and awareness

Sukhdev takes great pains to stay apprised of the various investment risks and market developments by reading financial publications, attending investment seminars and seeking professional advice from financial specialists. His knowledge enables him to make sound investment decisions while managing his risks effectively.

Conclusion

Sukhdev's case study illustrates the value of risk management to Indian investors. Through strategies like asset allocation, risk assessment, research and due-diligence reviews, regular portfolio reviews, use of risk management tools, maintenance of an emergency fund, adoption of diversification strategies as well as continuing his education on investment, Sukhdev has successfully mitigated and safeguarded his investments from risks while growing and stabilizing them over time. These practices contribute significantly towards long-term portfolio stability, resulting in steady long-term growth of Sukhdev's investment portfolio.

Key takeaways from this section

1. Increase your active income
2. Create multiple sources of income
3. Increase passive income
4. Reduce or defer expenses
5. Manage loans to avoid high interest costs
6. Minimize all leakages, like fees, insurance costs, etc.
7. Manage your risks

Section 6: Navigate (N)

'The best investment you can make is in yourself.'
—Warren Buffett

Finally, it must be said that navigating the complex world of personal finance can be challenging. It is important to seek out resources to help you make informed decisions. Consider joining a financial support group or working with a financial adviser to help you navigate the complexities of personal finance.

To navigate your financial planning journey efficiently, especially in the Indian context, an array of tools, resources and books are available to help you. They span areas such as investment planning, tax planning, retirement planning, insurance, estate planning and cash flow management, all of which are elements of the broader financial planning sphere.

Chapter 17

Knowledge Sources

Financial blogs

Financial blogs can serve as an invaluable resource for both the novice and the seasoned investor. They offer articles covering all areas of personal finance and investing, from mutual funds and stocks to insurance, tax planning and retirement planning. These blogs help their readers better comprehend complex concepts while staying current on trends and news in the sphere of finance.

Here is a selection of some well-known financial blogs in India and a short description of each:

1. **BasuNivesh:** Managed by Basavaraj Tonagatti, this blog provides financial planning advice, investment tips and information about various insurance products. BasuNivesh's blog is a valuable source for understanding the financial basics.
2. **JagoInvestor:** Created and run by Manish Chauhan, JagoInvestor offers investment advice and personal financial tips through articles covering mutual funds, insurance policies, loans and tax planning.
3. **Subramoney:** Authored by P.V. Subramanyam, an experienced finance expert with decades of industry

knowledge, this blog offers valuable advice on wealth management, retirement planning and personal finances, along with guidance on behavioural finance.

4. **Safal Niveshak:** Vishal Khandelwal's Safal Niveshak blog specializes in value investing principles. With an abundance of resources for investors to understand the subtle complexities of value investing, Safal Niveshak provides essential education in this area of investment.

5. **Capital Mind:** Capital Mind provides in-depth analyses of India's financial market scene. Covering topics like stocks, bonds, mutual funds and personal finance, this resource makes for a useful guide when seeking comprehensive market analyses.

6. **FreeFinCal:** Launched by Professor Pattabiraman from IIT Madras, FreeFinCal provides an innovative financial planning system using scientific methods for retirement planning and personal finance management.

7. **Relakhs:** Led by Sreekanth Reddy, Relakhs provides information on financial planning, investment, tax preparation services, income tax return filing and home loan financing. With an emphasis on personal and investment planning, this blog specializes in personal finance.

8. **A Wealth of Common Sense:** Written by Ben Carlson, this blog features wealth management strategies, personal financial advice and historical financial analyses. Even though the focus of this global blog lies outside India's borders, Indian investors can still gain a lot of insight into market philosophy and investing principles from it.

9. **GetMoneyRich (GMR):** Manish Choudhary's blog provides information and tools related to stocks, mutual funds and real estate investing as well as personal

finance tips and calculators to facilitate the planning of investment strategies.

10. **Three Longs & Three Shorts:** A weekly blog maintained by Marcellus, this curates articles on financial, technological, social, trends and others that are shaping the world. The blog contains a collection of three long articles and three short articles.

These blogs offer different points of view and types of financial advice, making them a comprehensive resource for anyone aiming to increase their knowledge of financial planning and investing.

News portals

Staying abreast of the financial news and market trends is critical to effective financial planning. News portals provide updated reports on the economy, markets, companies and financial instruments, as well as analyses from industry experts that can aid you in making informed investment decisions.

Here are the top financial news portals in India:

a) **Moneycontrol:** As one of India's premier financial news websites, Moneycontrol offers comprehensive coverage of the financial news, brings you market data, personal finance advice and portfolio management tools as well as live television shows on finance and investing.

b) **The *Economic Times*:** One of India's premier financial news sources, the *Economic Times* offers coverage of a wide variety of subjects such as market news, economic policy discussions, personal finance and wealth issues, as well as providing updates on IPOs, mutual funds and taxes.

c) ***Business Standard***: *Business Standard* offers news on multiple sectors such as the economy, policy, companies, personal finance and the financial markets and also provides in-depth analyses, opinion pieces and interviews with industry leaders.

d) **Livemint:** Livemint offers a comprehensive range of news and articles on finance, economics, investment and personal finance. The platform regularly reports stock market trends, provides in-depth analyses of current events that affect financial planning and also offers advice on how to improve your finances.

e) **CNBC TV18 in India and Online Portal:** CNBC TV18 offers real-time financial market coverage as well as business information to Indian audiences through its online portal that features news updates, analysis tools and expert advice for the audience to utilize.

f) **NDTV Profit:** NDTV Profit is an award-winning news source covering business, markets, the economy and personal finance. In addition, real-time stock market updates and interactive features can also be found here.

g) **BloombergQuint:** BloombergQuint is a joint venture between Bloomberg and Quintillion Media that provides business, economic and finance news with analysis and insights. It also provides live TV broadcasts and podcasts.

h) **Zee Business:** Zee Business provides financial news covering personal finance, market updates and business developments as well as expert analyses on investment and financial planning strategies.

i) **Financial Express:** *Financial Express* covers news
    on finance, markets, industry trends and personal
    finance. It provides a range of information, from
    personal budgeting advice to interviews with
    industry experts.

j) **Hindu BusinessLine:** Part of The Hindu family
    of publications, this publication covers the news
    from various sectors, including agriculture and
    agri-biz industries, as well as on economic, market
    and financial planning issues. It also carries expert
    analyses and opinion pieces from industry leaders
    and financial advisers.

Each financial news portal in India boasts different advantages,
so a range of resources would provide the most complete picture
possible of India's financial landscape.

Financial books

Financial books offer in-depth knowledge on a wide array
of finance-related topics. They can provide you with the
information and tools required to fully grasp complex concepts
like investing or financial planning strategies while offering
insights into the global markets and economies.

Here are some popular books that will give you an
understanding of the financial landscape, both international
and domestic:

1. Robert Kiyosaki's *Rich Dad Poor Dad*

This should be required reading for anyone seeking to
gain new perspectives on money and investing. Kiyosaki
compares and contrasts two men he knew—his own father
(fiscally poor) and a friend's father (financially wealthy).
By describing their parallel lives, he illustrates the need for

financial literacy, independence and the building of wealth through investments such as real estate holdings, company ownership or by the use of financial protection strategies.

2. Benjamin Graham's *The Intelligent Investor*

Benjamin Graham, widely recognized as the father of value investing, provides investors with approachable, foundational knowledge and philosophy on investing. In particular, the book highlights long-term strategies focusing on the purchase of stocks and bonds below their intrinsic value. His 'Mr Market' allegory provides guidance in understanding market fluctuations while making sound investment decisions. Warren Buffet, who had studied under Graham, has described this work as the 'best book on investing ever written'.

3. Vivek Mashrani's *You Can Compound*

Vivek Mashrani provides a comprehensive framework for equity investing, combining the principles of fundamental and technical analysis for screening the right stocks and an easy allocation strategy to ride the winning positions and cut the losing positions.

4. P.V. Subramanyam's *Retire Rich: Invest Rs 40 a Day*

This book emphasizes the significance of retirement planning and explores how small daily investments can accumulate into an impressive corpus upon retirement. Subramanyam emphasizes the power of compound interest over time and the necessity of asset allocation, all the while stressing how important it is to start investing early in India. This book should be required reading for anyone looking to understand India-specific retirement strategies.

5. P.V. Subramanyam and M. Pattabiraman's *How You Can Achieve Financial Security Through Goal-Based Investing*

This book serves as an essential guide to goal-oriented financial planning and investing, offering investors step-by-step assistance to identify their financial goals, select investment products that match these objectives and avoid common investing errors. With specific relevance for Indian markets and contexts, this book is particularly helpful to Indian investors.

6. Christopher H. Browne's *Little Book of Value Investing*

Browne offers an accessible yet comprehensive introduction to value investing, from how to purchase stocks quoting below their intrinsic value to which companies to avoid when waiting for potential opportunities and being patient enough when the right ones present themselves. This book serves as an indispensable reference tool for anyone attempting to adopt value-investment approaches in stock trading.

7. George S. Clason's *The Richest Man in Babylon*

This classic financial tale offers timeless wisdom through parables set in ancient Babylon. The lessons are about saving a part of your income, avoiding debts, making money work for you and investing it wisely in what interests you. These are principles that apply worldwide, although the book's scope doesn't directly and specifically include Indian finance.

8. Manoj Arora's *From Rat Race to Financial Freedom*

This book guides the reader from working for money to making their money work for them. It offers an effective road map towards attaining financial freedom by getting out of debt, saving, investing and planning for retirement.

It is especially useful for those stuck in their 9-to-5 jobs seeking financial independence.

9. Manish Chauhan's *16 Personal Finance Principles Every Investor Should Know*

This book breaks down complex financial concepts into easy-to-digest principles that provide the basis of sound financial planning, such as understanding one's cash flow, creating an emergency fund and planning for retirement.

10. Monika Halan's *Let's Talk Money: Now That It Is in Your Control*

Monika Halan, an esteemed finance professional, presents this helpful guide on managing money and investing wisely. The book demystifies financial planning, spanning topics ranging from health insurance and home loans to systematic investment plans and direct plans within mutual funds—everything needed for smart investing!

11. Napoleon Hill's *Think and Grow Rich*

This classic self-help book explores not just personal finance but rather how a mindset for financial success must exist in one. Hill shares insights gained after twenty years of researching the lives and careers of some of the wealthiest individuals of his day.

12. Amar Pandit's *The One and Only Financial Planning Book That Will Ever Be Needed*

Renowned financial planner Amar Pandit has penned this comprehensive book covering all the basics of financial planning, wealth management, risk mitigation and retirement planning in the Indian context.

13. Dave Ramsey's *The Total Money Makeover: Classic Edition: A Proven Plan for Financial Fitness*

Ramsey provides an easy and proven plan to pay off debt, save money and invest to achieve financial fitness in this classic book. Its principles apply globally.

14. Deepak Shenoy's *Money Wise: Timeless Lessons on Building Wealth*

Deepak Shenoy from Capitalmind provides a step-by-step guide on how to create wealth in his trademark simple style. The book is easy and fun to read and at the same time is a treasure trove of information about Indian markets and their working.

Each book in this list offers invaluable knowledge and advice regarding financial planning and investing, equipping you with tools to navigate the world of finance and ensure your future security. Remember: learning finance and investment is a lifetime journey, so keeping yourself updated on the market trends and news can only serve to benefit you.

Podcasts

Podcasts are a convenient and accessible means of expanding your financial knowledge. Their topics of discussion range from investing and personal finance, tax planning and market trends to interviews with industry professionals who share their advice and experiences.

Here is a selection of India's most popular financial podcasts, which can provide invaluable financial knowledge, give you knowledge of different approaches to investing and different perspectives on money management:

1. **Paisa Vaisa:** Hosted by Anupam Gupta, Paisa Vaisa is an interactive podcast covering various financial matters, including personal finance, investing, banking and economic affairs. It often features interviews with industry leaders or entrepreneurs.

2. **Capitalmind Podcast:** Hosted by Deepak Shenoy, founder of Capitalmind, this podcast offers in-depth analysis of and commentary on topics spanning market trends, personal finance, economic events and much more. It stands out for being very engaging.

3. **Equity Sahi Hai:** This is a podcast hosted by Motilal Oswal and serves to inform investors on the equity markets, mutual funds and related investment topics. Each episode includes discussions on pertinent themes by industry professionals.

4. **Moneycontrol podcast:** Moneycontrol, one of India's premier financial information sources, runs a podcast which delivers all the latest updates and expert commentary related to business, the market, the economy and personal finance in the form of daily updates and expert insight sessions.

5. **Paisa Paisa Kahe Hum:** Prakhar Gupta hosts this podcast that seeks to demystify complex financial concepts in Hindi, making this an excellent source for anyone searching for financial knowledge in Hindi.

6. **Meri Kahani:** BloombergQuint's Meri Kahani podcast showcases discussions by business leaders and market veterans. The content is quite motivating for budding investors and entrepreneurs.

7. **Market Wrap:** Moneycontrol's Market Wrap podcast gives listeners a daily recap of market events and the key headlines of the previous trading day; plus a preview of what to expect on the trading days ahead.

8. **ETMarkets podcast:** This helps you to stay current on the Indian stock markets. The ETMarkets podcast provides daily stock market updates and news related to the markets, business and the economy.

Each of these podcasts can offer you unique insights into financial planning, investment strategies and market trends. Listening to a variety of podcasts can help broaden your perspective when it comes to finance and deepen your understanding of financial concepts and strategies.

Online Courses

Online courses can provide structured and in-depth knowledge of financial planning and investing. They cover a range of topics, including personal finance, stock market investing, mutual funds, financial analysis and more. These courses are often created by industry experts or academic professionals and can help you gain a solid understanding of financial planning.

Coursera, Udemy and TechnoFunda Investing Academy offer several online courses on finance and investing. The National Institute of Securities Markets (NISM) and the National Stock Exchange (NSE) also offer several certification courses related to financial markets and securities trading.

Financial planners and advisers

Financial planners and advisers provide personalized advice based on your financial goals and situation. They can help you define your financial goals, develop a financial plan and guide you in making investment decisions.

You can find certified financial planners (CFPs) in India who are regulated by the Financial Planning Standards Board (FPSB) India.

Financial forums and communities

Forums and online communities are a great way to get real-world insights, get your questions answered and discuss topics related to financial planning.

Here are some popular financial forums and communities in India:

1. **Reddit—IndiaInvestments**: The IndiaInvestments subreddit is a community of investors discussing stocks, bonds, mutual funds and other forms of investment in the Indian context. It's a useful resource for insights from fellow investors and finance enthusiasts.
2. **Traderji**: Traderji is a forum that focuses primarily on the Indian stock market. Here, members share their experiences, ask questions and discuss topics related to stock trading, commodities, forex and other investment avenues.
3. **ValuePickr**: ValuePickr is a forum dedicated to the principles of value investing. It's a collaborative stock-picking and tracking platform where you can learn from other experienced value investors.
4. **TechnoFunda Investing Community**: This is a forum where investors collaborate and grow together by sharing information and learning about investing using technical analysis and fundamental analysis.
5. **RupyaGyan**: Although not a forum in the traditional sense, RupyaGyan has a section where users can post questions and get responses from the community. It focuses on personal finance and investment planning.
6. **Facebook groups**: There are various Facebook groups like 'Asan Ideas for Wealth', 'Common Sense Living' and 'Indian Stock Market', which discuss financial planning, wealth creation and investment.

7. **The Wall Street Oasis (WSO)**: While WSO is not India-specific, it does have a significant number of users from India. It's primarily for finance professionals and aspirants, covering topics such as investment banking, private equity and financial modelling.

8. **Quora**: Quora has several topics related to financial planning, investing, tax planning and personal finance in the Indian context. You can ask questions and get answers from the community.

9. **CAclubindia Forum**: This forum is especially beneficial for chartered accountants and finance professionals in India. It covers a wide range of topics, from taxation and auditing to personal finance and investment.

Remember that while these communities can provide you with valuable insights, the information shared should not be considered as the ultimate financial advice. It's essential to do your own research or consult a certified financial adviser before making financial decisions.

Government and regulatory websites

Government and regulatory websites provide accurate and official information on regulations, policies and guidelines related to financial planning and investing. They also provide resources like calculators, forms and guides, which can assist you in your financial planning journey.

The Indian government and its financial regulators run a host of websites that offer valuable resources and services for financial planning. Here are some of the authorities that run the most popular ones:

1. **Reserve Bank of India (RBI)**: RBI, India's central banking institution, regulates the monetary policy

with regard to the Indian rupee. It's the go-to source for policy updates, banking norms, interest-rate announcements and more.

2. **Securities and Exchange Board of India (SEBI)**: SEBI is the regulator of the securities market in India. It provides regulations, guidelines and useful resources for investors. It also hosts investor education programmes and allows for the filing of complaints against companies and intermediaries.

3. **Income Tax Department**: The official website of the Income Tax Department of India provides information on tax laws and policies, income tax returns, tax deductions, tax slabs and various tax-saving instruments.

4. **Ministry of Finance**: Its website is a source of information related to the country's financial and economic policies, budgets, economic surveys, foreign exchange rates and government treasury bills.

5. **Employees' Provident Fund Organization (EPFO)**: The EPFO website allows you to check your Provident Fund balance and transfer and withdraw funds. It also provides updates on new rules and regulations related to the Provident Fund.

6. **National Securities Depository Limited (NSDL)**: NSDL is an Indian central securities depository. Its website allows you to check and manage your demat account, gives you tax information and more.

7. **Insurance Regulatory and Development Authority of India (IRDAI)**: IRDAI is an autonomous body tasked with regulating and promoting the insurance and re-insurance industries in India. Its website contains information on insurance policies, regulations and guidelines.

8. **Public Provident Fund (PPF)**: Its official website provides information on PPF, a long-term investment

option offered by the Government of India. It also provides information on interest rates, withdrawal rules, loan facilities and more.

9. **National Pension System (NPS) Trust**: NPS Trust's website provides detailed information about the National Pension System, a voluntary retirement savings scheme. It allows subscribers to check their fund balance, change fund managers and adjust their portfolios.

10. **India Post Payments Bank (IPPB)**: The website of this outfit offers information on various savings and investment schemes, like National Savings Certificates, Kisan Vikas Patra, Sukanya Samriddhi Account and more.

Social Media

Social media platforms can be a great resource for financial learning and insights. Financial influencers and experts on social media platforms can provide you with regular updates, insights and tips on financial planning and investing if you follow them.

Platforms like Twitter, LinkedIn and YouTube have many financial influencers who regularly share valuable content.

In summary, there are numerous resources available that can assist you in navigating your financial planning journey in the Indian context. It's important to remember that while these resources can provide valuable information and guidance, you should also do your own research and consider your personal financial situation and goals when making financial decisions for yourself. Financial planning is a lifelong journey that requires continuous learning, discipline and patience.

Chapter 18

Financial Planning Tools, Software and Apps

Financial planning software and apps can help you manage your finances and investments more efficiently. They can help you track your income and expenses, manage your investments, plan your financial goals and monitor your financial progress.

1. **Zerodha's Coin and Kite:** Zerodha, a prominent stockbroker in India, provides 'Coin' for direct mutual fund investments and 'Kite' for trading stocks, ETFs and bonds.
2. **Moneycontrol**: This platform provides in-depth financial news, market data, analysis and investment tracking tools. It also allows users to manage their portfolios, monitor their financial goals and get investment advice.
3. **Paytm Money**: A platform developed by Paytm, India's leading digital payment service provider, Paytm Money offers a variety of financial services. It provides an online platform for investing in mutual funds, trading in stocks, ETFs and the National Pension System (NPS). It offers SIP (systematic investment plan) options for mutual funds and provides investment advice based on users' financial goals and risk tolerance.

4. **ET Money**: ET Money is a comprehensive financial planning app that enables users to invest in mutual funds, manage expenses and buy insurance. The app provides insights into users' spending patterns, helps them in budgeting and offers bill payment reminders. It also features tax-saving investments and health insurance plans.

5. **Groww**: Groww is a user-friendly investment platform that offers investments in mutual funds, stocks and digital gold. Users can track their portfolio performance, get regular market updates and receive personalized investment suggestions. It also provides educational content to help users understand financial planning better.

6. **CAMS**: As a service solution provider to mutual funds and other financial institutions, CAMS offers a dedicated online platform where investors can view their investments in multiple mutual funds through a single window. The platform allows for transactions like purchase, redemption and the switching of units within schemes.

7. **Smallcase**: Smallcase is a platform that enables investors to invest in portfolios of stocks or ETFs based on specific themes, ideas or strategies. It helps investors align their investments with their beliefs, financial goals or preferred investment strategy.

8. **Screener**: Screener is a stock analysis and screening tool that helps you view the financials of a company in a comprehensive, easy-to-understand format. It helps investors make informed decisions by providing key financial data, ratios, charts and other company-specific news.

9. **Cleartax**: Cleartax is an online tax preparation and filing platform. It offers a user-friendly interface through which individuals can file their income tax

returns (ITR) in a hassle-free manner. It also provides services like tax savings, mutual fund investments and GST software.

10. **Quicko**: Quicko is an online tax planning and filing tool that caters to individuals and businesses. It allows for seamless ITR filing, provides tax optimization strategies, helps in GST compliance and offers a variety of accounting solutions.

11. **BankBazaar**: BankBazaar is an online marketplace for financial products. It offers a platform where users can compare loans, credit cards and insurance from various banks and financial institutions and apply for them. It provides users with customized quotes based on their financial profile.

12. **Paisabazaar**: Similar to BankBazaar, Paisabazaar is an online financial services platform where users can compare, select and apply for a wide range of financial products like loans, credit cards and insurance. It also offers free credit score checks and provides investment options in mutual funds.

13. **Value Research Online**: Value Research Online is a resource for information and advice on mutual funds, stocks and personal finance. It provides in-depth analysis, detailed fund information and various tools for comparison and portfolio tracking.

14. **Goalwise**: Goalwise is a goal-based online investment platform. It helps users define their financial goals, calculates the investment needed for the same and then suggests funds to invest in. It also provides automatic rebalancing and goal-tracking features.

15. **NSE Paathshala**: This is a virtual trading and investment interface provided by the National Stock Exchange (NSE) of India. It is a platform where one

can learn about investing in the stock market, in futures and options, and in commodities.

Each of these tools/apps offers unique advantages and features tailored to various investment strategies and financial planning needs. Whether you are a seasoned investor or just beginning your journey in the financial markets, these tools can equip you with the necessary knowledge and resources to make informed decisions. They enable you to acquire greater control over your finances and help you manage your money more effectively and ultimately achieve your financial goals.

Key takeaways from this section

1. Keep yourself updated by reading financial blogs, news portals and books
2. Keep yourself updated by listening to podcasts
3. Invest in yourself by learning the financial nuances through an online course
4. Seek help and advice from qualified planners and experts
5. Follow government and regulatory agency websites
6. Follow social media to know of the latest happenings
7. Invest in tools and automation to make your investment journey easy and save time

Putting It All Together

'That's the whole secret: Earn more, spend less and automate it.'

—Tony Robbins

1. Assess your total income
2. Increase your active income by investing in skilling yourself
3. Create multiple sources of income, like blogs, podcasts, etc.
4. Increase your passive income through investments
5. Increase your passive income through rental income from residential or commercial property
6. An increase in income need not mean an increase in lifestyle expenses
7. Don't rely solely on one source of income
8. Focus on earning more income than on spending more money
9. Increase your investments as your income increases
10. Assess your total expenses
11. Categorize your expenses under Needs, Desires and Dreams
12. Defer your expenses falling in the Dreams and Desires buckets

13. Track your expenses to identify where there is potential for saving
14. Reduce expense leakage from unwanted subscriptions or recurring expenses
15. Pay bills on time to avoid late fees
16. Spend less than you earn
17. Negotiate for better deals and discounts
18. Be cautious of impulse purchases
19. Practice the thirty-day rule to reduce impulse buying. Wait thirty days before making a non-essential purchase
20. Practice mindful spending by evaluating each purchase based on its value and need
21. Maintain a good balance between spending and saving
22. Save first and then spend
23. Maintain two accounts; one for expenses and the other for investments
24. Set up automatic transfers from your salary account to your investment account
25. Set up an investment account for windfalls or unexpected cash inflows to avoid frivolous spending
26. Create a budget to know your income and expenses
27. Create a 'fun money' budget category to prioritize leisure/experience activities without overspending
28. Use online platforms or apps to track your expenses and financial goals
29. Review and negotiate your recurring expenses, such as on phone and Internet services
30. Implement an 'expense fasting' challenge for a designated period to reduce unnecessary expenses
31. Assess your total assets
32. Assess your total liabilities
33. Assess your risk profile and risk persona
34. Save a fixed percentage of your income regularly

35. Know your net worth
36. Invest in a healthy lifestyle or in wellness programmes to reduce long-term healthcare costs
37. Start investing as early as possible
38. Equity investments come with their downside; get used to it
39. The longer the investment period, the less the downside when it comes to equity investments
40. Learn to be comfortable with risk
41. Compound interest is the EIGHTH wonder of the world
42. Diversify your investments to minimize risk
43. Be mindful of hidden fees/costs when making financial decisions
44. Pay attention to investment fees and performance charges
45. Invest using the direct mutual fund purchase option
46. Invest in low-cost index funds for long-term growth
47. Invest in tax-efficient options like tax-free bonds and NSCs to minimize tax liability
48. Invest in precious metals like gold or silver as a hedge against inflation
49. The house that you live in is a place and not an investment
50. Look for simplicity in financial planning and investment advice
51. Avoid complicated financial instruments that you don't understand
52. Compare your progress to your plan; not to others' earnings
53. Don't make emotional investment decisions
54. Insurance is NOT an investment. Prefer term insurance policy over endowment policies
55. Avoid get-rich-quick schemes

56. Return of capital is more important than return on capital. Avoid high-risk investments

57. Focus on increasing the investment amount rather than focusing only on returns from capital

58. Minimize usage of credit cards

59. Embrace a cash-only approach for discretionary spending to stay within budget

60. Avoid high-interest loans like credit card overdues and loans from peer-lending platforms

61. Rank your loans and pay off high-interest-rate loans first

62. Avoid taking unnecessary loans

63. Build an emergency fund to cover three to twelve months' expenses

64. Invest your emergency fund in highly liquid assets like cash, bank accounts or FDs

65. Assess the size of your term insurance regularly

66. Purchase term insurance coverage to secure your family's future

67. Purchase a personal medical insurance cover

68. Consider top-up medical insurance for your family

69. Don't invest more than 10 per cent of your net worth in acquiring depreciating assets

70. Don't take loans to acquire depreciating assets

71. Develop a debt payoff plan using the snowball or avalanche method

72. Review your investments on a monthly cadence

73. Re-balance your assets on an annual basis

74. You don't have to be rich to invest

75. Invest today by saving even 5 per cent of your income

76. Aim for a savings rate of 20 per cent

77. Increase your savings amount annually by 10 per cent

78. Start a systematic investment plan (SIP) in equity/MFs to benefit from rupee cost averaging and long-term wealth creation

79. Setting up SIPs can accelerate the achievement of your financial goals
80. Leverage loss harvesting to save on income tax
81. Stay updated on tax laws and deductions
82. Consider the impact of taxes on investments
83. Have well-defined financial goals using the SMART framework
84. Prioritize and rank all your financial goals
85. Have a long-term financial plan which captures your goals, risk profile and asset allocation
86. Be mindful of your financial health as well as physical health
87. Invest in wellness and mindfulness to enjoy the wealth
88. Create a will and a succession plan
89. Seek professional financial advice when needed
90. Understand the impact of inflation on your savings and future goals
91. Stay informed about changes in the financial regulations
92. Your financial plan must account for major life milestones like education, wedding and retirement
93. Don't forget to invest in your relationships and social connections
94. Practise regular decluttering and sell unused or unwanted items to generate extra income
95. Practise gratitude and contentment in your financial journey
96. Invest in your personal and professional development
97. Prioritize life-long learning when it comes to financial education by reading books, attending webinars or joining online communities like TechnoFunda
98. Find an accountability partner to build discipline to achieve your financial goals
99. Explore refinancing options for loans to take advantage of lower interest rates

100. Contribute to charity regularly. According to Tony Robbins, giving is the ultimate secret to wealth, even though it sounds counterintuitive

Bonus Lessons

101. Plan and prepare for your financial independence. Buy health insurance when you are healthy, invest in a retirement fund while you are young
102. Simplify your financial planning by using apps or automating tools
103. Simplification of financial planning also makes active and regular management of your finances easy
104. Apply what you learn. Knowledge is useless if it remains only in the brain
105. Have a clearly defined financial plan
106. Ensure your asset allocation aligns with your goals and risk profile
107. Review and rebalance the plan. Review monthly and rebalance your plan annually
108. Patience and discipline are the two virtues needed to achieve your long-term financial goal once your plan is in place. Don't let emotions mess up the plan

Review this list regularly so that these lessons become your habit!

Financial Planning Flowchart: ACTION

- **Assess** current financial situation
  - Assess income and expenses
  - Categorize expenses under Needs, Desires and Dreams
  - Calculate savings (income – expenses)
  - Assess assets and liabilities
  - Calculate net worth (assets – liabilities)
  - Assess your risk profile and risk persona

- **Create** a Plan
  - Make SMART goals
  - Categorize goals based on their time horizon
  - Prioritize goals
  - Determine the cost of goals, accounting for inflation
  - Determine the investment instruments based on the required time horizon and risk profile
  - Determine the savings needed for each goal
  - Allocate savings to goals based on their priority
    - Drop or defer low-priority goals
  - Plan for contingencies
    - Emergency funds and Insurance
  - Plan for succession

- **Take Action**
  - Create a budget
  - Finalize your goals based on priorities and savings
  - Allocate the assets based on goals and risk profile
    - Choose the right debt instruments
    - Choose the right equity instruments
    - Diversify in gold, real estate or ReIT, InvIT
  - Create an investment plan based on goals and asset allocation
  - Execute your portfolio using the right platform
  - Track your portfolio regularly

- **Inspect Progress**
  - Review your Income, Expenses, Assets and Liabilities regularly
  - Review your goals semi-annually
  - Review your risks annually
  - Review your asset allocation annually
  - Rebalance your portfolio annually

- **Optimize**
  - Increase your sources of income
  - Increase your sources of passive income
  - Defer or reduce expense and liabilities
  - Manage loans to avoid high interest cost
  - Minimize leakages like fees, insurance, cost
  - Manage your risk

- **Navigate**
  - Keep yourself updated by reading financial blogs, news portals and books
  - Keep yourself updated by listening to podcasts
  - Invest in yourself by learning the financial nuances through online courses

o Seek help and advice from qualified planners and experts
o Follow government and regulatory agency websites
o Follow social media to know the latest happenings
o Invest in tools and automation to make your investment journey easy and save time

Glossary

1. **Alternative Investment Funds (AIFs):** Diversified investment pools employing non-traditional assets and strategies, offering investors unique opportunities and risk profiles beyond conventional stocks and bonds.
2. **Annual percentage rate (APR):** APR represents the annualized interest rate charged on loans, credit cards and other forms of lending products and represents the total cost of a borrowing.
3. **Arbitrage:** This term refers to taking advantage of price differences across markets or exchanges to make an immediate profit without much risk or financial loss.
4. **Asset allocation:** This refers to the practice of diversifying investments across asset classes such as stocks, bonds, gold and cash in order to achieve an ideal risk/return balance.
5. **Asset management company (AMC):** An outfit that manages and oversees investment vehicles such as mutual funds or ETFs on behalf of investors.
6. **Balanced fund:** A mutual fund that invests in both stocks and fixed-income securities to maximize both capital appreciation and income generation.
7. **Bear market:** A market marked by sustained price decreases associated with pessimism and selling pressure.
8. **Blue-chip stocks:** Shares of established, financially sound companies that boast of consistent performance and bring reliable dividend payments over time.

9. **Bombay Stock Exchange (BSE):** Prominent stock market facilitating the trading of securities, pivotal for capital formation and economic development in India.

10. **Bond:** A debt instrument issued by governments, municipalities or corporations to raise capital by paying periodic interest and returning the principal upon maturity.

11. **Bull market:** A market marked by sustained price gains associated with optimism and buying pressure.

12. **Capital gains:** The profit realized upon selling capital assets such as stocks, bonds or real estate. It is calculated as the difference between the selling price and the purchase price.

13. **Capital Gains Account Scheme (CGAS):** Tax-saving initiative in India enabling individuals to defer capital gains tax on property transactions, promoting financial flexibility.

14. **Capital gains tax:** A form of tax levied on profits generated from selling certain assets such as stocks, bonds or real estate.

15. **Capital market:** A financial marketplace where long-term securities, such as stocks and bonds, are bought and sold.

16. **Certified Financial Planners (CFPs):** Accredited professionals offering comprehensive financial planning services, guiding clients towards achieving their financial goals with strategic and personalized advice.

17. **Commodities:** These are raw materials or primary agricultural products, such as gold, oil, wheat, etc., that can be bought and sold.

18. **Compound interest:** Interest earned from the initial principal plus the accumulated interest from prior periods.

19. **Computer Age Management Services (CAMS):** Tech-driven provider streamlining mutual fund services, ensuring efficient administration and operational support in the financial industry.

20. **Consumer Price Index (CPI):** Benchmark measuring average changes in prices of goods and services, crucial for assessing inflationary trends in an economy.

21. **Credit score:** A score that measures an individual's creditworthiness according to their history and repayment behaviour; lenders use it as an assessment of risk when offering credit to potential borrowers. It is a number that ranges from 300 to 900. A score below 550 is regarded as very poor while a score above 700 is regarded as good.

22. **Currency futures:** Financial contracts that allow individuals and institutions to buy or sell currencies at predetermined prices on future dates at predetermined costs.

23. **Deposit Insurance and Credit Guarantee Corporation (DICGC):** Safeguard for bank depositors in India, providing insurance coverage and financial security in case of bank failures.

24. **Derivatives:** Financial instruments with values derived from the underlying assets such as stocks, bonds, commodities or currencies.

25. **Direct equity:** An investment strategy where one buys individual stocks or shares of companies directly for ownership purposes keeping in mind their potential for capital appreciation.

26. **Dividend:** A distribution of cash or additional shares from the profits of a company paid out to shareholders.

27. **Dividend yield:** This financial ratio is the annual dividend per share divided by the current market price. It provides an estimate of the return on investment (ROI).

28. **Electronic Debt Bidding Platform (EBP):** Online marketplace enhancing transparency and efficiency in debt security trading through electronic bidding.

29. **Employee Provident Fund (EPF):** This scheme, mandated by the Indian government for employees, is a retirement

savings scheme where part of the employee's salary is deducted and accumulates in an EPF account.

30. **Employees' Provident Fund Organization (EPFO):** Administrative body managing provident funds and pension schemes for employees in India, promoting long-term savings and retirement benefits.

31. **Environmental, Social, and Governance (ESG):** Criteria evaluating a company's ethical and sustainable practices, influencing investment decisions for socially responsible portfolios.

32. **Equated Monthly Instalments (EMIs):** Regular fixed payments made by borrowers towards loan repayment, ensuring systematic and predictable debt servicing.

33. **Equity:** Ownership interest in a company, represented by shares or stocks, providing rights to the shareholder in terms of voting, dividends and capital appreciation.

34. **Equity-linked savings scheme (ELSS):** A type of mutual fund offering tax benefits under Section 80C of the Income-tax Act for long-term capital appreciation opportunities.

35. **Exchange-traded fund (ETF):** A fund that tracks a particular index or sector and is traded on the stock exchanges.

36. **FIMMDA Trade Reporting and Confirmation System (F-TRAC):** System in India for transparent trade reporting and confirmation in the fixed income market, enhancing operational efficiency.

37. **Financial adviser:** An independent professional who offers impartial guidance and advice on investment, insurance policies, retirement planning strategies and wealth management to individuals or businesses.

38. **Financial Planning Standards Board (FPSB):** Establishes ethical standards for certified financial planners, ensuring quality and integrity in financial planning services.

39. **Fixed deposit (FD):** A financial instrument whereby an individual or entity deposits funds with a bank for a fixed period with a predetermined interest rate.

40. **Fixed Income Money Market and Derivatives Association of India (FIMMDA):** Association overseeing development and regulation of fixed income, money markets and derivatives markets in India.

41. **Forward contract:** Here, the contracting parties agree between themselves to purchase or sell an asset at an agreed-upon price at some future date.

42. **Fund of Funds (FOFs):** Investment strategy involving mutual funds that invest in other funds, providing diversification across various asset classes.

43. **Gold Accumulation Plans (GAPs):** Structured plans allowing systematic investment in gold, providing an alternative method for owning the precious metal.

44. **Gold exchange-traded fund (ETF):** An exchange-traded fund that tracks gold prices to offer buyers exposure to the commodity without requiring actual physical ownership of gold bullion or bars.

45. **Goods and Services Tax (GST):** Unified indirect tax system in India, streamlining taxation on goods and services for economic efficiency.

46. **Government Securities (G-SEC):** Debt instruments issued by the government, considered secure investments due to government backing.

47. **Green bond:** A fixed-income investment instrument where the investments involved are in projects that are of environmental benefit, such as renewable energy generation or energy efficiency initiatives or climate adaptation projects.

48. **Growth fund:** Some mutual funds offer growth funds that invest solely in stocks or securities with the intention of producing long-term capital appreciation; others specialize in growth funds that invest for long-term capital growth by purchasing stocks with potential long-term value appreciation.

49. **Hindu Undivided Family (HUF):** Legal term denoting a joint family structure under Hindu law, with shared assets and income among family members.

50. **Holding company:** A corporation that owns majority shares in other entities and exerts direct control over their management and operations.

51. **Holding period:** It refers to the length of time an investor holds a particular investment, such as stocks or bonds, from the time of purchase to the time of sale. The holding period is a critical factor in determining the tax implications of capital gains or losses.

52. **House Rent Allowance (HRA):** Component of salary compensating employees for housing expenses, enhancing overall compensation packages.

53. **Housing loan:** Loan provided by banks or financial institutions to individual borrowers or entities for the purchase or construction of residential property.

54. **Income Expenses Assets and Liabilities (IEAL):** Components of financial statements representing an entity's financial position through income, expenses, assets and liabilities.

55. **Income Tax Returns (ITR):** Annual declarations submitted to tax authorities, disclosing income details for tax assessment purposes.

56. **Index fund:** An index fund (also referred to as an exchange-traded fund, ETF or mutual fund) seeks to replicate the performance of an index such as the Nifty 50 or the BSE Sensex.

57. **India Post Payments Bank (IPPB):** Banking services provided by India Post, extending financial services through its vast postal network.

58. **Inflation:** The steady and widespread increase in prices across goods and services that diminishes purchasing power over time.

59. **Inflation rate:** The annualized percentage change in a price index over a particular time frame.

60. **Infrastructure Investment Trusts (InvITs):** Investment vehicles channelling funds into infrastructure projects, offering investors exposure to income-generating assets.

61. **Initial public offering (IPO):** The sale of shares by a private firm to raise capital and become publicly listed.

62. **Insurance Regulatory and Development Authority of India (IRDAI):** Regulatory authority overseeing the insurance sector in India, ensuring fair practices and protecting policyholders.

63. **Interest rates:** They measure either the cost of borrowing money or the returns you get from investments, expressed as an annual percentage.

64. **Leave Travel Allowance (LTA):** Employee benefit covering travel expenses during approved leave, supporting work-life balance.

65. **Liquid fund:** An asset-class of mutual fund that invests in short-term money market instruments with high liquidity; it is ideal for parking surplus funds in and for meeting short-term financial goals.

66. **Liquidity:** The ease with which an asset can be converted into cash without impacting its market price. It indicates the potential of the asset to be bought or sold with minimal price impact.

67. **Money market (or financial asset exchanges):** The market for short-term debt instruments with high liquidity and minimal risk, to be bought and sold quickly in the open market or on the exchanges themselves.

68. **Mutual fund:** An investment vehicle that pools money from numerous investors into one portfolio handled by professional fund managers.

69. **Mutual Fund Utilities (MFU):** Platform streamlining mutual fund transactions, offering a centralized solution for investors and fund houses.

70. **National Institute of Securities Markets (NISM):** Educational institution providing training and knowledge in securities markets, contributing to financial education.

71. **National Pension System (NPS):** A voluntary retirement savings scheme, it is an initiative introduced by the Government of India offering individuals tax advantages and flexible investment choices.

72. **National Savings Certificate (NSC):** Government-backed savings bond in India, offering secure investment with fixed returns for savers and investors.

73. **National Securities Depository Limited (NSDL):** It facilitates electronic holding and transfer of securities in India, enhancing efficiency in the securities market.

74. **National Stock Exchange (NSE):** India's premier stock exchange for stocks, derivatives and other financial instruments.

75. **Net asset value (NAV):** A mutual fund's net asset value per share is calculated by dividing the assets minus the liabilities by the number of outstanding shares.

76. **Non-banking financial companies (NBFC):** Financial institutions that offer banking services, such as loans and investments, without possessing an official banking licence.

77. **Peer to Peer (P2P):** Direct lending and borrowing between individuals, facilitated through online platforms, enabling decentralized financial transactions.

78. **Portfolio Management Services (PMS):** Professional management of investment portfolios, offered to high-net-worth individuals for customized investment strategies.

79. **Prepayment:** Repaying loans or debt before their scheduled maturity dates often leads to savings on interest payments and reduces the total cost of debt over time.

80. **Primary market:** A marketplace where newly issued securities, such as stocks or bonds, are offered and purchased by initial investors.

81. **Provident Fund (PF):** Mandatory retirement savings fund for employees, contributing to financial security after retirement.

82. **Public Provident Fund (PPF):** An investment vehicle introduced by the Indian government offering individuals tax advantages and a competitive fixed interest rate over time.

83. **Real estate investment trust (REIT):** An investment vehicle that owns and manages income-producing real estate properties for investment. Investors gain exposure to this sector of the real estate market.

84. **Recurring deposit (RD):** An investment account where individuals can regularly make deposits over an arranged time frame at an agreed interest rate.

85. **Reserve Bank of India (RBI):** Central banking institution in India, responsible for monetary policy and financial stability.

86. **Risk management:** The practice of identifying, assessing and mitigating any potential risks in an investment instrument or business so as to limit losses or adverse repercussions.

87. **Rupee cost averaging:** An investment strategy wherein a sum of money is consistently invested at regular intervals in something in an attempt to minimize fluctuations and keep average purchase prices constant over time.

88. **Rupee-dollar exchange rate:** The exchange rate between the Indian rupee and the United States dollar. It represents their values relative to one another.

89. **Securities and Exchange Board of India (SEBI):** India's regulatory body responsible for overseeing the securities markets, protecting investor interests and encouraging the development of the capital market.

90. **Sensex:** The benchmark index of the BSE, which includes thirty of India's biggest companies by market capitalization.

91. **Sovereign Gold Bonds (SGBs):** Government securities denominated in grams of gold, providing an alternative to physical gold ownership.

92. **Specific, Measurable, Achievable, Relevant and Time-Bound (SMART):** Goal-setting framework for effective planning and achievement.

93. **Stock exchange:** A regulated marketplace where traders and investors purchase and sell securities such as stocks and bonds.

94. **Stock market indexes:** These statistics measure a selection of stocks that provide an indicator of the overall market or a particular sector's performance.

95. **Systematic investment plan (SIP):** A method of investing in mutual funds wherein regular contributions of an equal sum are made to encourage disciplined and sustainable investing practices.

96. **Tax deduction:** An expense or amount that can be deducted from an individual's taxable income to reduce his or her overall tax bill and thus the overall tax liability.

97. **Tax planning:** This practice of organizing financial affairs and transactions to minimize tax liability within the framework of applicable tax laws can significantly lower tax liabilities for individuals and businesses.

98. **Technical analysis (TA):** An approach for assessing securities and predicting their price movements using historical price/volume information, chart patterns and statistical indicators.

99. **Technical default:** A situation in which a borrower fails to adhere to the non-financial covenants or conditions specified in the loan agreement and breaches it by failing to fulfil those commitments.

100. **Term insurance:** Life insurance that offers coverage for an agreed-upon term period and pays out death benefits should the insured die during that term period.

101. **Underwriting:** This refers to assessing and accepting the financial risks associated with insurance policies or investment offerings.

102. **Unit-linked insurance plan (ULIP):** An insurance-cum-investment product that provides life-insurance protection while giving investors access to various investment funds.

103. **Volatility:** The level of variation or fluctuation in the price of a financial instrument, indicating its degree of risk or uncertainty.

104. **Wealth management:** Wealth management services offer tailored financial planning, investment management and other advisory services for high-net-worth individuals or families.

105. **Whistleblower:** An individual who discloses any illegal or unethical activities within an organization that breach the laws or regulations; typically, these activities involve fraud, corruption and violations of the regulations.

106. **White-label ATMs:** Non-bank entities operating ATMs that provide cash withdrawal and basic banking services on behalf of partner banks.

107. **Yield curve:** A graphic depiction of interest rates across bonds or securities with different maturities, showing the relationship between interest rate and time to maturity.

Scan QR code to access the
Penguin Random House India website